P

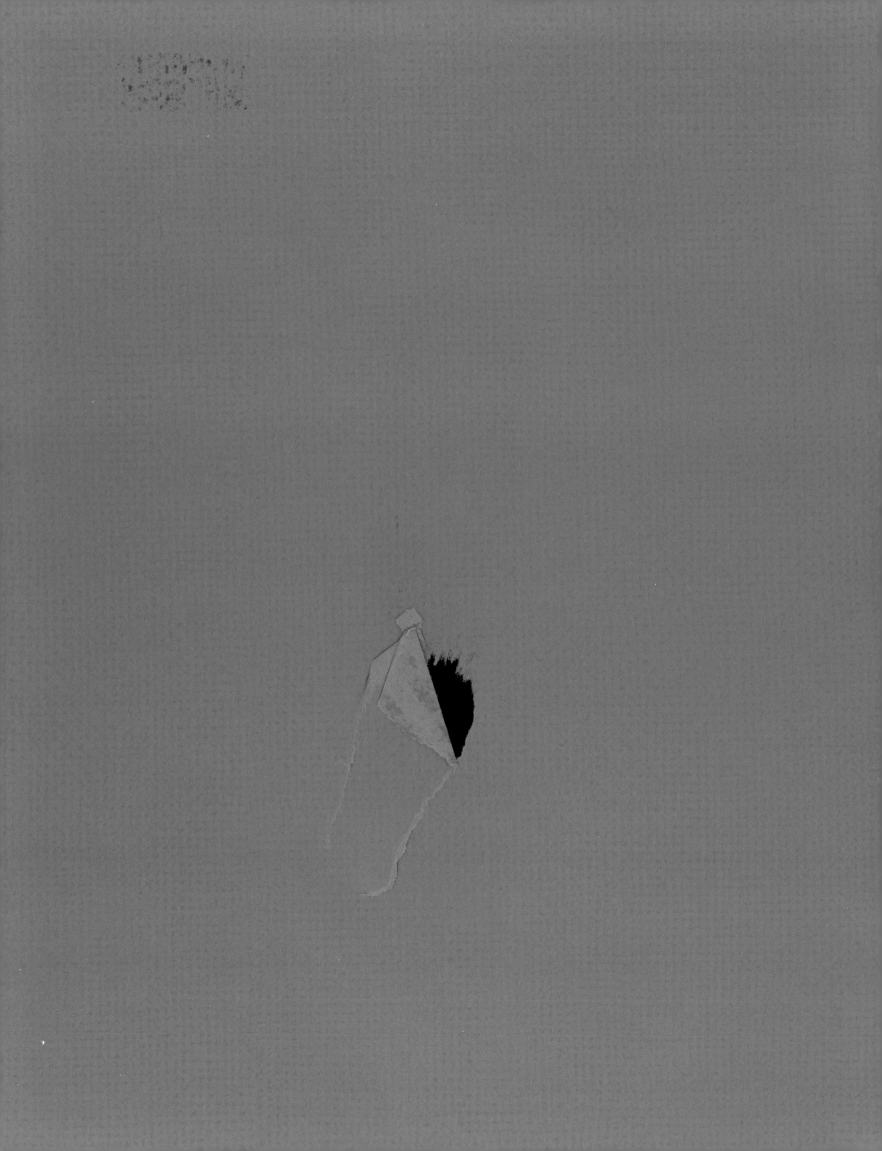

Children
of the
North

Children
of the
North

by Fred Bruemmer

OPTIMUM PUBLISHING COMPANY LIMITED
Montreal · Toronto

Other Books by Fred BRUEMMER

The Long Hunt. 1969

Seasons Of The Eskimo. 1971

Encounters With Arctic Animals. 1972

The Arctic. 1974

The Life Of The Harp Seal. 1977

Published by Optimum Publishing Company Limited,
Montreal

Legal deposit - 4th trimester 1979
Bibliothèque nationale du Québec

For information, contact:
Optimum Publishing Company Limited,
Michael S. Baxendale, Director,
245 rue St.-Jacques,
Montreal, Quebec
H2Y 1M6

ISBN 0-88890-095-3

Printed and bound in Canada

Contents

Foreword

During my first year as Governor General of Canada, I have had the opportunity to satisfy a strong, personal interest in Canada's native peoples by visiting many of Canada's northern communities. I have been able to observe first hand the way of life in our Arctic and, I trust, have gained a better understanding of a unique and intriguing culture.

It is unfortunate that other Canadians will not have a similar chance to explore this region of our country. I am happy to be able to say, therefore, that through the years, Fred Bruemmer has been instrumental in allowing *all* Canadians to discover their North. Once again, through the words and photographs of his books, he has, in this International Year of the Child, created a portrait of the children who live in that region. The publication of this work is his distinctly Canadian contribution to this year's world-wide celebration of youth. This book *Children of the North* will give the world an opportunity to recognize and understand a relatively unknown group of children and the difficult challenges which they face as they prepare for a rapidly changing future.

Even more importantly however, this work may also, for the first time, alert many Canadians to the problems of the new generation of the North.

Increasing this type of knowledge is important to Canada, for, as you will discover as you progress through Mr. Bruemmer's work, the children of the North are a generation at a cross roads. They bear the imprint of two very different cultures and cannot easily abandon one for the other. Nor should they be expected to. If it is not now too late, they should rather be allowed to incorporate the modern with the traditional, so as not to be totally absorbed by southern ways.

These children face a formidable challenge and the way will not be easy. But it will be infinitely easier if southern Canadians learn more and try to understand and appreciate the life of northern Canadians.

It is my hope that readers will seriously reflect upon the contents of *Children of the North* and will gain an increased awareness and understanding of a unique group of Canadians. And, by so doing, I hope that we will be convinced that the continuation of the distinct culture of the Inuit should be encouraged and welcomed as an essential part of the fabric of our nation.

Ed Schreyer C.C., C.M.M., C.D.
Governor General of Canada

on board the C.G.S. icebreaker
Louis S. St. Laurent off Nanasivik,
September 19, 1979.

With love and affection

for all

The Children Of The North

and

for my own two boys

Aurel and René

Credits
Editors: Paul Rush, Anna Ozvoldik
Design: Ian Black, Suzanne Vincent Poirier
Cover photo of Fred Bruemmer by Michel Gravel
Type: Poppl Pontifex by Avant-Garde Ltée, Montreal
Production: Mary Doyle, Mary Rigby, Linda Watson
Printed by The Bryant Press Limited, Toronto

Eskimo fathers and sons set out on a hunting trip in the morning.

Preceding page:
Eskimo of the central Arctic
travelling by dogteam in a
spring night.

The father builds the igloo, the
sons fill the chinks with snow.

A little Eskimo girl from the
central Arctic wears warm and
fluffy mittens made from arctic
hare fur.

Far left:
Dressed in clothes made of caribou fur, a little boy from Bathurst Inlet is well protected from
the arctic cold.

A little girl waits while her father builds an igloo, shelter for the night during an extended
trip.

A little girl from Igloolik.

Far left:
An Eskimo boy from Baffin
Island.

17

A Vanishing Way of Life

To southern man, raised on the Biblical precept that only "the rod and reproof give wisdom," and who, in turn, applied plenty of both to his offspring, the children of the north were an unceasing source of wonder. They were never beaten and rarely reproved. Yet instead of turning into little hellions, they were, by and large, pleasant, polite, and obedient. Amazement at this runs like a refrain through the annals of arctic literature. Greenland's Eskimos, wrote the Danish missionary Hans Egede in 1771, "never make use of whipping or hard words to correct [their children] when they do anything amiss, but leave them to their own Discretion. Notwithstanding which, when they are grown, they never seem inclined to Vice and Roguery, which is to be admired."

In Siberia, the 19th century Swedish explorer Baron Nordenskjöld noted that Chukchee children "are never chastised nor scolded. They are, however, the best behaved I have ever seen. Their behavior in the tent is equal to that of the best brought up European children in the parlor."

At Point Barrow in Alaska in 1881 the anthropologist John Murdoch observed that among the Eskimos "the affection of parents for their children is extreme, and the children seem to be thoroughly worthy of it. They show hardly a trace of fretfulness or petulance so common among civilized children, and though indulged to an extreme extent are remarkably obedient. Corporal punishment appears to be absolutely unknown, and children are rarely chided or punished in any way. Indeed they seldom deserve it; for in spite of the freedom which they are allowed, they do not often get into any mischief..."

Mrs. Tom Manning who lived with her naturalist husband among the Eskimos of southern Baffin Island in the 1930s found that "children are rarely scolded or corrected for any fault. It is a mystery to me how they grow up to be, for the most part, such charming people, obedient, cheerful, courteous. We met a family of white children at Pangnirtung who were reputed to be 'little demons' before their arrival in the north. After continued association with Eskimo children, however, they had become polite and well-mannered."

And thirty years later the Canadian author Sheila Burnford was equally charmed with the Eskimo children at Pond Inlet on northern Baffin Island who "were the most happy, self-contained and naturally courteous little people that I have ever met."

These observations, far removed from each other in time and space, are remarkably similar and dozens of others, virtually identical in tenor, could be added. They all agree the children of the north are charming, well-behaved, and obedient, paragons of virtue, but quite happy ones, fortunately. What they fail to mention is how such admirable results were achieved. The process is subtle and usually fairly gentle but effective as I found out on my first long trip in the north.

It was in Norwegian Lapland, in spring a number of years ago. In the valley where I lived with Nils Aslakson Siri and his family it was already warm. Rivulets of meltwater gurgled down the slopes. We were on the eve of the great spring migration with Nils' reindeer herd across the vast vidda, the great inland plateau of tundra and moor, to the northern coast, where the reindeer would spend the summer. Everyone was busy. The children helped to prepare provisions and pack the sleds. Nils looked critically at my outfit. "You will need warmer clothing, especially fur boots. It will be cold on the vidda," he said. I demurred. My clothing, I thought, was wholly adequate for the trip. Nils didn't argue. He just went on with his work.

It took only a few days for me to find out just how right Nils had been. Icy winds swept across the immensity of the treeless vidda. While the others sat warmly muffled on the reindeer-drawn sleds, I trotted alongside, chilled and repentant.

One evening the wind ceased. It became intensely cold, a world of hushed, crystalline magnificence. The great reindeer herd moved urgently northward, wreathed in the misty vapor of the animals' frozen breath, like a dark, shifting mirage in the bluish, diaphanous frost haze of the night, beneath a deep-ochre sky. It was beautiful and strangely dream-like but, beset by pain and self-pity, I was oblivious to it. The snow was hard; it creaked and shrilled beneath the sled runners. We travelled fast and I ran for hours, trying desperately to keep my feet from freezing. "Cold?" Nils asked, a faint smile on his dark face. I nodded, miserable and contrite, and trudged on.

When we finally camped, I was utterly exhausted. I crawled between layers of reindeer pelts and fell instantly asleep. When I awoke, a beautiful pair of new fur boots, a warm jacket and fur trousers lay next to me. "For you," said Anna Christina, Nils' wife. They had evidently been made for me before we left and had been kept for just the right moment. Deeply grateful I put them on and for the rest of the trip I was warm, happy—and obedient.

Nils and his wife had treated me exactly as they would have treated an obstreperous child. Let him have his way. And if, as a result, he suffers, let him suffer. It does wonders for the learning process. Just watch that he doesn't get badly hurt. Rub it in a bit and the lesson will be remembered.

Guided, advised, and unobtrusively but persistently cajoled by loving parents, the children of the north not only became polite and obedient, they also learned to accept and endure the hardships and difficulties that were so often part of life and travel in the Arctic.

In the fall of 1913, Vilhjalmur Stefansson's expedition ship, the *Karluk,* was caught by ice north of Alaska and drifted toward destruction. Aboard were 25 persons, sailors, scientists, and an Eskimo family: Kureeluk, his wife Kiruk and their two small girls, Helen, 11, and Mugpi, 3. After the ship sank, they made a nightmare journey over the ice, across belt after belt of pressure ridges, some of them more than 100 feet high, to reach Wrangel Island, north of Siberia. "The children were no bother at all. I cannot remember, through all our ordeals, ever hearing one of them cry," William Laird McKinley, one of the survivors of the trip, recalled. "The children never seemed to be affected by the cold or any of the hardships which laid low strong white men." Eleven of them died, but the children and their parents survived.

There were three children on our trip across Lapland's vidda: a baby, Per Olaf, 7, and Inga, 11. The baby, plump and placid, slept most of the time tucked into its cozy "komsa," the Lapp cradle, beautifully carved from a piece of birch log and lined with down-soft fawn fur. Per Olaf was a stout little boy, round, ruddy-faced, voracious and bubbling over with life and energy. Inga was strikingly beautiful, her sloe-eyed, strong-boned, dark-complexioned face topped by a thatch of straw-blond hair. She was hard-working, happy, gentle and motherly.

The rhythm of our life was dictated partly by weather but mainly by the migratory urge of the reindeer. As long as the herd marched northward, we followed with our long caravan of reindeer-drawn sleds. When the herd finally stopped to rest and browse, we camped. Nils and I set up the "kota," the tall, tee-pee-shaped tent. Anna Christina unloaded the sleds. Per Olaf and Inga lugged pelts, sacks and boxes to the tent. Then they were off to get firewood, digging out the creeping dwarf birch from underneath the snow. The chil-

20

dren tugged at the tough, resilient branches and sprawled backwards into the snow when they suddenly snapped. They laughed and giggled, their faces glowing in the frosty air. The pile of branches grew bigger and bigger. They heaped them on a sheet of canvas and hauled them to the tent, then trotted back for the next load. In an hour-and-a-half they had collected enough wood to last us the night.

Anna Christina baked pancake-like unleavened bread in a soot-blackened cauldron suspended by a chain above the fire in the center of the tent. Inga played with the baby. She hugged it, tickled it gently and, when the baby crooned, wobbled its fat little chin so the crooning changed into a moist burble. Per Olaf whittled the short spears we needed to roast slivers of dried reindeer meat over the fire. He used his mother's "buiko," the slightly upcurved, razor-sharp Lapp dagger, with alarming verve but considerable skill. Scars on his dark, pudgy hands showed the skill had been painfully acquired. When he was finished, he joined Inga and they both played with the baby. It was the adored and pampered pet of the whole family. There was a warm, relaxed feeling of harmony and happiness in the tent. One day it stormed. The vidda vanished in

the whirling white of wind-driven snow. Anna Christina repaired clothing. Inga sewed a pair of boots. Her mother had cut the fur pieces for her in the intricate, traditional pattern, and now she sewed them together with thread made of dried, twisted reindeer sinew, the stitches close and neat. Per Olaf ate. That was his favorite occupation. Then he crept between the reindeer pelts and slept. In the evening the storm grew worse. Somewhere out there in that white void was Nils, always near his herd. The reindeer were his entire wealth and he got little sleep or rest during the migration. The canvas clattered against the poles and the wind moaned and wailed around our tent.

Anna Christina told stories, mostly the ancient tales of Stalo, the hairy, hungry monster that prowls the wintry woods, searching for nice, fat Lapp children to take home, boil and eat. But he is a dumb brute and the cunning children always escape. The themes were ancient, universal; they crop up in the tales of many lands, but here their setting was uniquely Lapp. Stalo surprises a group of children (they have been disobedient and have gone far from home, despite their parents' warnings) and stuffs them into his sack. On the way to his lair he gets tired, sits down and falls asleep. One boy has his buiko along. He slits the sack, they spill out, fill the sack with rocks and a girl, who carries needle and thread, sews up the hole. Stalo awakes, lugs home the sack, huffing, puffing and famished, and boils an enormous pot of water. When he empties the sack, the rocks splash into the boiling water and Stalo and his greedy wife are scalded.

In another tale, Stalo catches a boy, but before he can get around to eating him, the boy tricks him into a contest: to squeeze water out of a rock. Stalo grabs a stone and crushes it to dust between his huge, hairy hands. But there isn't a drop of water. The boy picks up a stone, presses it and water dribbles down. It is really a chunk of cheese which he had in his pocket and quickly substituted for the stone. Stalo, as usual, is the loser.

And so the tales continued, far into the night: the tough, wily little Lapps outwitting the fearsome, lurking ogres. The children listened, enthralled. They probably knew many of the stories, for a couple of times Inga added small details her mother had omitted. The fire crackled and hissed, its light flickered across the dark faces. Strangely distorted shadows danced upon the sloping, smoke-grimed walls of the tent. And outside the storm raged on.

That was some years ago. Now most Lapps escort their reindeer herds with snowmobiles, and their families travel to the coast by bus or car. The ancient land-bound, nature-linked cultures of the northern peoples are being rapidly eroded and supplanted by cultural and technological influences from the south. Ancestral skills are discarded, centuries-old traditions abandoned. Among Canada's Eskimos, said the Oblate priest Maurice Metayer, "the elders were the living books of the traditions, legends and exploits of their people ...[but] the art of the story-teller is almost lost in the Inuit [Eskimo] villages today." The ancient tales fade into oblivion.

For eons the cultures of the northern people persisted, timeless and nearly immutable. The traditions and verities of one generation became, unchanged, those of the next. Frank T'Seleie of Fort Good Hope echoed this when he told Mr. Justice Thomas R. Berger during the inquiry into the proposed natural gas pipeline along Canada's Mackenzie valley: "Our Dene [Indian] nation is like this great river [the Mackenzie]. It has been flowing before any of us can remember. We take our strength, our wisdom and our ways from the flow and direction which has been established for us by ancestors we never knew, ancestors of a thousand years ago. Their wisdom flows through us to our children and our grandchildren, to generations we will never know."

It was a hard life, often haunted by the gaunt spectre of famine. February in the language of the Aleuts was known as "qisuginax," [the month of the] last stored food, and March as "qadugix qisagunax," [the month] when one eats thongs and skins. Peter Freuchen told of a Polar Eskimo woman in northwest Greenland whose husband had drowned. She and her four children were caught in a terrible famine. To spare the children the excruciating, lingering death by starvation, she hanged them. (The Eskimos regarded this as a sublime act of mother love.) But one boy asked not to be hanged and promised he would not complain, no matter how dreadful the suffering became. He survived by eating rabbit droppings and grass. He remained small and stunted, but he was fast and immensely enduring and later became a famous hunter whose descendants live to this day in the Thule region. His mother remarried and was known throughout the region for her passionate love of children. She "took care of all the young people in the settlement."

Life for the Eskimos in former days oscillated between dearth and plenty, hardship and happiness. They accepted the hard times with fatalistic resignation. "Ayornamat," they said, it cannot be helped. And they enjoyed to the utmost the good that life brought them. On his travels in the 1920s through arctic Canada, the famous Danish ethnologist Knud Rasmussen met an old Eskimo woman who had had a terribly hard youth because "I had always been a poor fatherless creature, passed from hand to hand." Then she married and that was "the end of all my adventures. For one who lives happily has no adventures, and in truth I have lived happily and had seven children." Then she burst into tears and when Rasmussen asked her why she was crying, she said, "I have today been a child once more... And I could not help crying for joy to think I had been so happy."

Theirs was a timeless, egalitarian society.

"...they knew nothing of days or weeks; they kept no reckoning even of the months, only of the changing seasons as they affected the food supply," the anthropologist Diamond Jenness noted on Victoria Island in 1914, where he lived with Eskimos who had just been "discovered." "Their language contained no word for any number beyond six." Individual independence, the freedom to do precisely as they liked or as the mood of the moment moved them, was one of the basic concepts of their culture and later, when their children had to go to school, they chafed at its regulations and restraints. In the 1940s a third-grader in Barrow, Alaska, wrote a touching little vignette about his friend Isaac (one pities both Isaac and his teacher): "Isaac sing too much. Isaac like to make noise in school. Isaac always funny in school. Isaac is slow when he write. Isaac and I like to play outside." And the biologist Sally Carrighar noted that Eskimo children in Alaska "....were finding it hard to adjust to the routine [of school]. It is typical of their race to become depressed if they have to do the same thing every day...The children are not defiant... They just have to be free."

Once they possessed a freedom which we in our time-and rule-bound societies can no longer even imagine. Eskimo society, Jenness noted in 1914, did "dispense with all authority and grant to the individual a freedom that was well-nigh absolute." The very ideas of servitude, of master and man, of the subjugation of one man's wishes to another man's will were totally alien to them. Their language does not even have a word for "obey." It was a cultural trait that white explorers found in turn admirable, baffling and exasperating. "They cannot be controlled," complained the American explorer I.I. Hayes, annoyed that Greenland's Polar Eskimos would not accept orders from him. "...the Esquimaux are each a law unto himself. They are the most self-reliant people in the world." On Baffin Island at the same time (1860) another American explor-

er, Charles Francis Hall, was also having problems with the free-spirited Eskimos. They were, he said, good companions and superb hunters but "...they will do just as they please ...utterly regardless of my wants or wishes. They mean no ill; but the Inuits are like eagles—untameable."

In order to live together in reasonable harmony, these supreme individualists, who acknowledged no law and brooked no interference, had to comply with certain standards respected by all. They had to be induced to willingly set the common weal above their private whims and wants. This was largely achieved by the power of tradition and public opinion. The anthropologist Jean Briggs who lived with a native family in an isolated camp in arctic Canada for more than a year, noted that Eskimos place "a high value on mildness and gentleness...control of temper is a cardinal virtue..." and the most "damning traits that one Eskimo can ascribe to another" were bad temper, stinginess and unhelpfulness. This general aversion to overt expressions of ill-temper was so ancient and ingrained in the Eskimo culture that in Greenland, in the 1850s, the Danish scientist Henry Rink observed with surprise that the language of the people was "devoid of any real words for scolding."

Social pressure was effective. The Polar Eskimos, said the explorer Elisha Kent Kane, "exist in both love and community of resources as a single family." Food, traditionally, was shared. Good hunters were known as the "large-handed men," for they provided food not only for

their own families but for those of others, less skillful or fortunate. Poor hunters were pitied and sometimes teased. But self-centred, niggardly men and women who avariciously hoarded food and failed to share it, were excoriated: "...public opinion formed the judgement seat, the general punishment consisting in the offender being shamed in the eye of the people," wrote Henry Rink.

Those who failed to conform to the tradition—hallowed mores of their society, were skewered on the rapier of ridicule, society's most potent weapon. In its simplest form this consisted of barbed gossip and in these tiny communities such acidulous remarks inevitably reached the offender and his family. To be ridiculed and despised was more than most could bear and they usually tried to improve and live according to the commonly accepted tenets of their society.

In addition to such informal needling, the Eskimos, especially in Greenland, used ridicule in a highly ritualized fashion. During festivals a considerable amount of time was devoted to "nith"—songs. These were lampoons, carefully thought out and structured, and presented in public. Such a nith-song often started innocuously enough: "Thinking of nobody in particular but people in general..." only to zero in with devastating satire on the failings of a certain person. Once the song was finished, the person upon whom scorn and ridicule had been heaped had his turn. The assembled villagers, loving every second of it, acted as arbiters. "The cheering or dissent of the assembly at once represented the judgement as well as the punishment," noted Henry Rink.

There once was a man in East Greenland notorious for being selfish and mean. He stored food beneath his bed and ate it privately, surreptitiously. Then he wrapped the remains of the food in skins and hid them again under his bed. He got his deserts at a festival when a fellow-villager sang the following nith-song which Rasmussen recorded:

"I put some words together,
I made a little song,
I took it home one evening,
Mysteriously wrapped, disguised,
Underneath my bed it went:
Nobody was going to share it,
Nobody was going to taste it,
I wanted it for me! me! me!
Secret, undivided!"

So shamed and humiliated was the miser by this song that he became one of the most generous members of the community.

In a society without laws or law enforcement such public airings of grievances had a powerful and beneficial cathartic effect. Repressed anger was released, accumulated bitterness dissolved in mutual laughter. Errant members made an effort to mend their ways. In this manner adults used ridicule to keep the behavior of other adults within socially acceptable norms. They used it with equal skill and success on their children to ensure that they behaved in desirable ways. Into this society with its ancient subtle checks and balances that permitted total individual freedom within a loose framework of tradition-sanctioned obligations, came the white man with different beliefs, different life styles, a different ethic, a totally different culture. The Eskimos instantly acknowledged the white man's supremacy in technology; he owned infinitely superior weapons and tools. In other realms the Eskimos were less inclined at first to admire or emulate whites, nor were the other peoples of the north favorably impressed by southern mores and modes of life. The Lapps, the Roman historian Tacitus had noted nearly 2,000 years ago, "are extraordinarily wild and horribly poor...they dress in skins, they sleep on the ground...Yet it is this people's belief that in some manner they are happier than those who sweat out their lives in the field, and wear out their strength in houses..."

Initially the Eskimos regarded white explorers with a mixture of fear, hostility, envy (for their material wealth) and plain wonder. In 1923 when Rasmussen visited the then still extremely isolated Utkuhikhalingmiut near Chantrey Inlet in the Canadian Arctic, they remembered members of the British Back expedition that had reached their region in 1833 as "...remarkable, smiling men, who walked about with lumps of wood in their mouths emitting smoke." On closer acquaintance, wonder often changed to contempt. Whites, they felt, were loud, overweening, inquisitive, demanding and tactless, all traits which Eskimo culture traditionally abhorred. The behavior of whites, which to them appeared boorish and boisterous, both frightened and repelled them. The famous Eskimo hunter, carver and diarist Peter Pitseolak of Cape

Dorset said of a disliked Eskimo that he was "just like a white man—bossing everybody." Typically, whites with their assertiveness and lack of self-control reminded them of little children. An old Netsilik Eskimo confided in Rasmussen in 1922..."It is generally believed that white men have quite the same minds as small children. Therefore one should always give way to them. They are easily angered, and when they cannot get their will they are moody and, like children, have the strangest ideas and fancies."

They may have been lacking in the social graces valued by Eskimo society, but whites had come to stay in the north and they brought with them, in addition to their disparate and soon dominant culture, a Pandora's box of lethal gifts. The Eskimos in their remote and frigid realm had been a remarkably healthy people. While traversing the Northwest Passage (1903-1906) the Norwegian explorer Roald Amundsen arrived at the "firm conviction" that "the Eskimos living isolated from civilization of any kind, are undoubtedly the happiest, the healthiest, most honorable and most contented..." And Diamond Jenness observed that "climate combined with isolation preserved the Eskimos' ancestors from most of the widely spread diseases...keeping them a wonderfully healthy people until the white man broke into their solitude." That contact was frequently catastrophic, for the long isolated Eskimos had little or no resistance to southern diseases.

In 19th century Alaska, the Eskimos, ravaged by illness, beset by rough and violent whalers, exploited by traders who were often ruthless and grasping, were "desperately struggling against a flood of calamities that threatened their total destruction," said Diamond Jenness. Between 1828 and 1890 the population of Point Barrow decreased from 1,000 to 100, that of Point Hope from 2,000 to 350, and at Shishmaref Inlet where once nearly 2,000 Eskimos lived, only three families were left. Within ten years of their discovery, one third of the Eskimos just east of the Mackenzie Delta had died of influenza, and of the survivors many were being slowly consumed by tuberculosis. Labrador's Eskimo population declined from 3,000 in 1750 to 750 in 1946. Explorers and whalers reached the Eskimos of southern Baffin Island in the 1840s. Twenty years later Charles Francis Hall noted sadly that these people were "fast dying out." To obtain the white man's superior and coveted goods that they soon came to regard as essential, most Eskimos became trappers. Their main item of trade was the skins of arctic foxes, a commodity whose availability was subject to the cyclic fluctuations of fox populations and whose value depended upon the caprice of fashion. The price of fox pelts rose from $2.50 in 1908 to $15 in 1914, to a phenomenal $63 in 1929, only to plummet abruptly to $30 in 1930, $8 in 1934 and $3 in the 1940s. "To rest the economy and welfare of a whole people on...trapping alone is not merely hazardous but criminal," wrote Diamond Jenness.

As ethnologist with Stefansson's expedition, Jenness had lived from 1913 to 1916 with Eskimos who had just been "discovered," and wrote about them with fondness and admiration. Forty-five years later he returned to the Arctic and was appalled by what he saw: "The Eskimos of today are a beaten people, bewildered by all the changes that have buffeted them since the beginning of the century, and unsure both of themselves and their future. Fifty years ago they looked the white man proudly in the face, considering themselves his superiors or at least his equals." Now most were living on welfare, mired in degrading dependency. "The once proud hunter has lost his freedom and independence...and is sunk in apathy."

Even prior to this, some white men in authority had already taken a hard, dispassionate look at the north, its future and its people and had decided (perhaps accurately) that the natives' land- and sea-based hunting economy was doomed. Southern men and their industries would invade the north in ever-increasing numbers. To compete with them on an equal footing and to obtain jobs the natives would have to acquire the white man's education, skills and motivations.

There wasn't much that could be done about the adults, but their children could be educated for this white man's future that southern administrators and educators foresaw for the north. It was usually done with the best of intentions, but the means employed were often deplorable, the results achieved often tragic.

Nearly a century ago in Alaska, the Department of the Interior decreed that "the education to be provided for the natives...should fit them for the social and industrial life of the white population of the United States and promote their not-too-distant assimilation... The children shall be taught in the English language...No textbooks printed in a foreign language [i.e. Indian or Eskimo] shall be allowed."

In Canada seventy years later, the aims were similar. Two scientists studying educational methods in the western arctic found that "educational and other officials are often quite candid in stating one of their goals to be the weaning of children away from traditional Eskimo community and culture." Delineating government policy an official proposed that "the best way to handle the...[native] problem was to maintain the adults on relief and separate their children in the school hostels...The young generation would thus fare well in the future, since they would have learned from the school behaviour and attitudes more appropriate for town life, without the disruptive influence of their parents." This was carried out and, in this society with its strong tradition ethic where, as the anthropologist Margaret Mead put it, "the past of the adults...[was] the future of each new generation," a chasm opened between the generations. Diamond Jenness tells of an

Two little Eskimo girls play with a small sled.

Preceding page:
A Polar Eskimo boy has gaffed a
Greenland halibut in a lead.

Opposite:
Late at night under a flaring
sun, the children return to camp.

The children have a sled and their playground is infinite.

A girl builds a little snow house.

A Cree Indian girl from a settlement on the coast of James Bay.

Far right:
A little girl at the tent door asks
to take the baby out.

While others pray during a service held at home, two Eskimo girls share a candy, passing it
from mouth to mouth.

An unhappy moment in a usually
happy life.

Far right:
An Eskimo girl on Little
Diomede Island in Bering Strait,
half-way between Alaska and
Siberia.

Eskimo boy who was raised in a mission boarding school. He lived there for several years and was then returned to his parents' camp. Jenness met him there in 1916, "a sad lonely boy, unfamiliar with [the parents'] way of life and unable even to converse with them except by signs." Fifty years later Jean Briggs was present at the isolated camp at Chantrey Inlet when a girl returned from a long stay in a far-away hostel. The parents listened in puzzled silence to their "daughter's tale of the strange Kapluna [white man's] world where people are always loud and angry...where they hit children, let babies cry, kiss grown-ups, and make pets of dogs and cats." Many young people recall their hostel existence with mordant bitterness. Dolphus Shae of Fort Franklin told the Berger inquiry: "Before I went to school the only English I knew was 'hello,' and when we got there we were told that if we spoke Indian they would whip us...We all felt lost and wanted to go home, and some cried for weeks and weeks ...Today I think back on the hostel life and I feel ferocious." Another young Indian told the same inquiry: "For myself, I find it very hard to identify with anybody because I have nobody to turn to. My people don't accept me any more because I got an education and the white people won't accept me because I'm not the right colour...I'm lost. I'm just sort of a person hanging in the middle of two cultures." They had become, in the words of one young Eskimo, "half people."

Alienated from their parents and their past, bewildered by a present which seemed to offer no secure and satisfying alternatives to their former existence and over which they had little or no control, their future hazy and hardly hopeful, many of the disoriented young, as well as their numbed and saddened elders, sought solace in alcohol. This in turn led to violence and crime. "There are already juvenile delinquents among Eskimos nowadays, something unheard of in the days before they attended school," noted the teacher Margery Hinds in 1960. And in 1975, Dr. Otto Schaefer of the Northern Medical Research Unit wrote: "The only social institution of major importance in Eskimo life—the family—is falling apart, and nothing has yet appeared to take its place. The individual is left lonely, frightened, without direction and full of anxiety." The result of this disintegration has been "the frightening prevalence of violence in recent years in which accidents, poisoning, homicide and suicide are identified as the principal causes of death among most native groups in the Northwest Territories, the Yukon, and Alaska."

In a reversal of former policy, courses in "native skills" now form part of the curriculum of most northern schools, and the children are taught in Eskimo by Eskimo teachers in the lower grades. Attempts are made to preserve the ancient culture, the "old way of life." To most it still holds a powerful allure; some families have left the settlements to return to the land. It may be a futile escape towards a past that cannot be resurrected, but the back-to-the-land movement persists.

In the summer of 1978 I stayed briefly at Kittigazuit, a white whale hunting camp at the head of the Mackenzie Delta facing the Beaufort Sea. It is an ancient camp site. Eskimos have lived there, and hunted white whales, for hundreds, perhaps thousands, of years. Now they use it only during the summer whale hunting season. An old man, his wife and their son and his family lived there. For fifteen years the old man had held a well-paying job, in Inuvik. He gave it up, built a log cabin near one of the delta arms, hunted, fished and trapped. His son and family had later joined him.

"Town life was easy," he said. "But it was not good. Too much drinking. Too much fighting. Too much trouble. Here, on the land, we are at home. We are poor, but we are happy again. We want our grandchildren to grow up as Inuit. We want them to know the old ways."

Nunassiaq: The Beautiful Land

The snow fell softly, evenly. Within minutes of leaving Qânâq, main settlement of the Polar Eskimos in northwest Greenland, we seemed to be travelling through an infinite void: nine dogs, one sled, four people, going from nowhere to nowhere in a world all white, suspended in time and space. The only sound was the slight creaking of the flexible sled as it slid smoothly over the wind-fluted snow. Masautsiaq guided his dogs with unerring certainty. The shape of snowdrifts, sculptured by prevailing winds, served him as compass.

We were bound for the floe edge, the limit of landfast ice, Masautsiaq, his wife Sofie and Arrutaq, their ten-year-old grandson. Masautsiaq, in his early sixties, was small and stocky, but very strong and agile, a hunter well-known for his skill and daring, yet modest and unassuming in the best tradition of the Polar Eskimos. He was a person of great charm and kindness, always polite, friendly and helpful, a truly gentle man. Sofie, several times grandmother, was an amazingly young-looking woman, her long hair glossy-black, her skin smooth, her figure lithe, her movements quick and supple. The first time I met them, I thought she was Masautsiaq's daughter, then lapsed into embarrassed silence when I discovered my faux pas. But Masautsiaq only smiled, amused and good-natured, and Sofie was absolutely delighted. Arrutaq's father had a job in Qânâq and could only hunt on weekends, so the boy often accompanied his grandparents.

We crossed Inglefield Bay, then travelled west on smooth ice, parallel to the coast, vaguely visible through the veil of gently falling snow. Masautsiaq told Arrutaq and me about the land. "That valley," he said, "is a good place to snare arctic hares"; "this bay is rich in sculpins and they are easy to catch in summer";

"over there, where you see the dark rocks, people once lived," and he told us who they had been and who their descendants were. Every bay had its story, each peninsula its legend, every hill and dale its descriptive name. "That flat area is called 'the place where one finds drill points,' because long, long ago people gathered flint chips there to make bits for their bow drills." We passed a small river, frozen now and covered with snow, its alluvial fan near the sea a chaos of dun-colored rocks. "If you follow this river inland for half a day," said Masautsiaq, "you come to two mountain lakes and they are full of landlocked char. The best time to catch them is in early winter."

We stopped at Natsilivik, to rest the dogs and to make tea. It is an ancient site. People had lived there for hundreds, perhaps thousands of years; the ruins of collapsed houses, once ingeniously built with cantilevered stone slabs, were everywhere. Now they were just mounds of rubble, partly covered by drifting snow. It looked bleak and cold. "Naduq grew up in this house," said Masautsiaq. "She is the wife of Inuterssuaq in Siorapaluk." On a rock shelf at the very edge of the frozen sea, lay a giant boulder, an erratic left eons ago by receding glaciers. People once stored food on top of it, out of reach of their voracious sled dogs. It still bore the black marks of congealed fat. "Long ago," said Masautsiaq, "there was a great fight here between the Eskimos and the Tunit. Our people attacked them. One of the Tunit fled to the top of the big rock, but an Eskimo shot him with an arrow and he fell down and died."

His folk memory spanned the ages. The Tunit were Dorset culture Eskimos, and the fight that had taken place at this spot and which Masautsiaq described to us in such vivid detail had occurred at least 800 years ago. His father had told him the story and some day Arrutaq would be telling it to his children. To Masautsiaq's immense store of knowledge about his land and his people, Sofie added the spice of gossip. Masautsiaq knew who had lived at every old camp site we passed along the coast. Sofie knew what the people who lived there had done and spun for us some juicy tales of passion and intrigue, embroidered perhaps, for she had a glowing imagination, but all the more memorable for that. Between Masautsiaq's host of facts and Sofie's flights of fancy, this land, so featureless and *triste* and dreary, all chalky-white and dun, came vividly to life, each place associated in our minds with names and tales and memories.

To southern man, the Arctic seemed an awful place. "The whole of the country...has so hard and severe a winter, that there prevails there for eight months an altogether unsupportable cold," wrote the Greek historian Herodotus nearly 2500 years ago. And the 17th century Italian priest Francesco Negri noted in wonder, "...no oats can grow there...no vines are there to provide men with drink...One night in this region may last no less than two months...The cold is of such rigour that for eight months of the year snow and ice cover all land and all water...as for summer, the air is noxious with mosquitoes and midges which come in such hosts that the sun is obscured. All this being so, one would surely hold that the country cannot be inhabited by so much as wild beasts...yet inhabited it is. For this land...[is] Lapland."

To northern man, his frigid realm seemed bountiful and splendid. "Nunassiaq," the Eskimos call it, the beautiful land. True, it is cold and the mosquitoes can be a nuisance, but the Eskimos look at the positive side of things, as in this little Eskimo song:

"Cold and mosquitoes
These two pests
Come never together."

"The Eskimos are themselves unaware of the difficulty of their existence," wrote Peter Freuchen. "They always enjoy life with an enviable intensity, and they believe themselves to be the happiest people on earth living in the most beautiful country there is."

In the 1930s, the anthropologist Edmund Carpenter told an Aivilik woman about the marvels of the south: its cities, its factories, its forests, its wealth, and its warmth.

"Are there many caribou?" she asked.

"None."

"Seal? Walrus? Bear?"

"None at all."

"Oh!" she replied in astonishment and pity.

In 1860, when Charles Francis Hall went to Baffin Island on the whaler *George Henry,* an Eskimo who had spent a year in the United States was aboard. Now Kudlago was eagerly looking forward to being home again. But he was sick and failing fast. North of Newfoundland he asked to be taken on deck. "His last words were 'tei-ko se-ko? tei-ko se-ko?' Do you see ice? Do you see ice?" He died before they reached the ice he so desperately wanted to see once more.

"As the sea is laying there, we look at it, we feed from it and we are really part of it," Norah Ruben of Paulatuk told the Berger inquiry. And Louis Caesar of Fort Good Hope added, "This land is just like our blood..." They loved their harsh and rugged land, they were a part of it. They knew its moods, they read its signs. "The Aleuts," said the Russian bishop Veniaminov who lived amongst them from 1824 to 1834, "observe the changes in the sky with such an intensity that this, in their expression, was known as talking with the sun and the sky."

To know the land was vital because they often travelled far. For the Eskimos of Baffin Island, noted the anthropologist Franz Boas in the 1880s, "journeys of four to five hundred miles in one spring are not of rare occurrence; longer journeys, however, frequently last for years." A travelling Eskimo is the most observant of men and he has a highly retentive visual memory. He notes the shape of a distant hill, the distinctive lichen patches on a prominent boulder, the meanderings of a brook, and years later he will recognize these features instantly. At Repulse Bay in 1921, Rasmussen gave an Eskimo "pencil and paper, [and] he drew, to my astonishment, the whole coastline from Repulse Bay to Pond Inlet (about 800 miles), without hesitation," in great detail and with near-total accuracy.

European and American explorers usually named geographical features in the north after royalty, expedition patrons, friends, themselves and fellow explorers. These names tell nothing about the land. Eskimo names are descriptive and mnemonic, containing concise information about distinctive aspects of each place. In the Repulse Bay region, the spot where the Matheson River debouches into Lefroy Bay is called "Mamiktuikto," (the place where) 'a river comes out of the ground which never freezes.' Cape Jermain is "Anangiaiuk," 'there are black spots on the rocks which look like flies.' Hoppner Strait is known by the highly specific word "Tutjat" which means 'where caribou pass through shallow water between the islands and the mainland

in summer.' Lyon Inlet is "Akrearongnak" because it 'looks like a stomach,' and Gore Bay is, if not elegantly then at least memorably named "Itiriuk," 'the anus'. From childhood on, an Eskimo memorized hundreds of names like these, forming in his mind a vivid mental map of a frequently enormous region. In the 19th century the Polar Eskimos of northwest Greenland lived in small camps, each with two or three families, scattered along more than 600 miles of coastline where "every rock has its name, every hill its significance," wrote the explorer E.K. Kane. And "throughout this extent of country every man knows every man."

They lived dispersed, specks of humanity upon the immensity of their land. They were independent and individualistic, yet intensely sociable. Three or four families might stay together for weeks, or months, or even years, then drift apart to hunt in other regions or join another group, each family an autonomous unit, free to follow its moods and its desires. They loved to visit and received visitors with joyous and often lavish hospitality. When Rasmussen and his Eskimo companions stopped at the home of Takornaq, an Igloolik woman, she composed, in sheer delight, a song:

"All is more beautiful,
All is more beautiful,
And life is thankfulness.
These guests of mine
Make my house grand."

Yet while they loved to be with others, essentially each family was sufficient unto itself. They had no rulers and no laws, land and sea belonged equally to all. They owed fealty to no man, no nation and no tribe. The family unit was the core and essence of their culture, the focus of their loyalties, the basis of every man's and every woman's happiness and fulfillment, the mould in which each new generation was shaped in the likeness of the one that preceded it. In a song, part poem and part prayer, an Eskimo man addressed the snow

high in the mountains above his camp:
"Little snowslide,
Four children and my wife are my whole
world, all I own, all I can lose, nothing can
you gain.
Snowslide, save my house, stay on your sum-
mit."
An Eskimo woman evoked her vision of happiness with this song:
"It is so still in the house.
There is a calm in the house;
The snowstorm wails out there,
And the dogs are rolled up with snouts under
the tail.
My little boy is sleeping on the ledge,
On his back he lies, breathing through his
open mouth.
His little stomach is bulging round—
Is it strange that I start to cry with joy?"
Many marriages, in the past, were arranged by
parents. This did not preclude a considerable
amount of prenuptial flirting and romancing.
Netsit, the great poet of the Umingmaktor-
miut at Bathurst Inlet, made a song about it
which Rasmussen recorded in 1924.
"Glorious it is
To see young women
Gathering in little groups
And paying visits in the houses.
Then all at once the men
Do so want to be manly,
While the girls simply
Think of some little lie."
But once a young pair was married, the bond
usually lasted, if not, at first, because of love,
then for the quite pragmatic considerations of
mutual need and interdependence. Their land
was harsh, their life hard. Hunting was a
fickle, time-consuming occupation. It required
long trips, endless patience, experience, a
great variety of skills and, in a land where
winter might last eight months and more,
expertly sewn fur clothing to withstand the
rigors of the climate. A single man remained a
dependent, looked after by his mother, or by
the wives of friends and relatives. In Eskimo

the words for "unmarried man" and "lonely
man" are synonymous. "If a man loses his
wife, he is immediately destitute," wrote Peter
Freuchen, and "a woman who loses her husband, is reduced to the state of a beggar."
Unable to provide for herself, a single woman
remained with her parents or, if they were
dead, with relatives, often resented, sometimes exploited, a sort of live-in drudge, an
object of pity and frequently of contempt.
Eskimo society did not encourage spinsterhood.
Marriage, whether by parental arrangement
or personal choice, was a simple affair. There
was no priest, no wedding, no ritual, no vows
and, in most groups, neither dowry nor bride-
price were required. The young people moved
in together and henceforth, in the eyes of
their society, were considered married. They
might, for a while, live with in-laws, usually
the groom's parents, but most quickly established a home of their own. That, too, was
simple. Building materials, stone, bone, snow,
sod and, in the western Arctic, driftwood were
plentiful and freely available. Regional
designs of house construction were traditional and varied little over the centuries.
George Best, chronicler of Martin Frobisher's
expedition, saw Eskimo homes on Baffin
Island in 1578: "From the ground vpward they
builde with whale bones, for lack of timber,
which bending one ouer another, are handsomely compacted in the toppe togither, &
are couered ouer with seales skinnes..." Half
the house was occupied by a raised sleeping
platform built of stones "whereon strawing
Mosse, they make their nests to sleepe in."
That sounds cute but is not accurate. Best
saw abandoned houses. In an occupied home,
the moss-strewn platform would have been
covered with a layer of pelts and the people
would have slept beneath voluminous fur
blankets. Such a winter house could be built
in a few days, an igloo in a few hours. In summer people lived in tents.
A house was constructed by husband and

wife. Pitseolak, the famous Cape Dorset artist, recalled that when her son got married, he and his wife built their own house and insulated it with layers of brush and sod. The young wife returned with a large load of twigs. "They were too heavy for her and she fell down, covered in bushes. They laughed. They were happy building their hut together." The winter houses of former days had windows made of scraped, translucent seal intestines and were heated by two or more halfmoon-shaped seal oil lamps, usually made of soapstone. Such houses, said Franz Boas, who lived in them in the 1880s on Baffin Island, were "very warm, light, and comfortable." And Stefansson, a bit given to hyperbole, wrote an entire chapter in one of his books about the *Tropical Life Of The Polar Eskimos.*

The young couple had few possessions. To a people who travelled much, a plethora of goods was a hindrance rather than an asset. A man needed hunting weapons, a knife, a few tools, a kayak and a sled. An Eskimo bride's trousseau, noted Diamond Jenness in 1914, consisted of "a meat-knife, a sewing-kit, a lamp and a cooking pot." Their movements were seasonal and many of their possessions were only needed at certain times of the year. Thus fishing gear was cached near the river where they usually caught char. Sled, winter clothing and winter tools were left near the winter camp. Travelling Utkuhikhalingmiut, Jean Briggs observed, leave a "wake of belongings" cached for future use on "convenient hilltop boulders." When I went by boat with an Eskimo from Wakeham Bay on Hudson Strait for a week-long trip to an island 60 miles away, I noticed that he did not have a tent along. "I left one on the island four years ago," he explained. Such scattered belongings were perfectly safe. Theft was extremely rare. "Among us it is only the dogs that steal," a Chantrey Inlet Eskimo told Rasmussen in 1923.

The man was the master of the household. He made all decisions. His authority was absolute. That, at least, was the outward appearance. In practice most Eskimo wives had plenty to say, only they said it quietly and in the privacy of their homes, taking care to maintain the culturally approved façade of male dominance. When Ekalun of Bathurst Inlet, with whom I lived for many months, went shopping at the Hudson's Bay Company store 50 miles from our camp, it was a fine display of lordly decisiveness. He marched from shelf to shelf and picked out the things he required. To me this was amusing because, since I lived with him, I happened to know that prior to the shopping trip he had been carefully programmed by Rosie, his wife. In the Eskimo household of former days, according to Freuchen's terse dictum, man was the mouthpiece, woman the brains. Alone they were two barely viable halves, together they formed a successful unit, the respective roles of man and wife quite disparate, but equally vital to their survival.

Man, essentially, was the provider, woman the keeper of the home. Man's foremost task was to hunt, to provide his family with food. In addition, he had to make all his hunting weapons and tools and keep them in good repair. He constructed the family house or igloo, he built his kayak and sled, and looked after the sled dogs and their harnesses. He made toys for his children and all the implements his wife required: needles of copper, bone, ivory or jade, and needle cases; skin scrapers; oil lamps; and the cooking pot, shaped like a miniature sarcophagus, "cutte and made of stone very artificially," as the Elizabethan chronicler George Best observed.

A woman's duties were equally demanding and diverse. She helped to build the house or igloo; she cooked all the meals. She raised, fed and clothed the children. She skinned the animals her husband brought back, cut up the meat and, in summer, dried part of it for future use. She pegged out skins to dry and later scraped them. She sewed all the clothing for her husband and herself and made sure that all clothes were properly dried and repaired each day. She kept the oil lamp filled, collected and dried the moss that served as wick and ensured that it burned with an even, soot-free flame. She chewed the family's footwear to keep it supple and comfortable. She made thread out of sinew and thimbles of leather. In summer she gathered firewood, in fall she collected berries. She helped to spear char, often nearly hip-deep in icy water; she split the fish and laid it out to dry and later helped to cache it. She was the first to rise, the last to go to bed.

It was a hard, work-filled existence, but it differed not that much from a woman's lot in other lands, in the "Merry England" of Shakespeare's time, for instance. There, according to a handbook of that period, a yoeman's wife, a person of considerable social standing, was expected to: keep the house clean; make the beds; work in the garden; make preserves; make and mend clothing; cook, weave and spin; raise children and livestock; milk the cows, make cheese, and butter in the churn; dip candles and make rushlights; and sell dairy products, fowl and pigs in the market. In addition to these and many other chores she had "...to winnow all manner

of corns, to make malt, wash and wring, to make hay, shear corn, and in time of need to help her husband to fill the muck wain or dung cart, drive the plough, to load hay, corn and such other...", and, as a rule, bear a child each year, only to see many if not most of them die.

Life for the people of the north was by no means all hardship and drudgery. In the spring of 1916, Diamond Jenness lived at an Eskimo fishing camp west of the Coppermine River. Char had been plentiful; the rocks near camp were covered with drying fish. "The natives, who had nothing to do except deposit their fish in caches as it dried, were lounging around their tents, enjoying the halcyon days of early summer...when life seemed a glorious holiday." The American engineer W.B. Cabot visited Labrador's Naskapi Indians in 1906 at Mistinipi Lake. The caribou hunt had been good, the people had ample food and ample leisure, and held drum dances nearly every night. "In such times of plenty the Indian life is peculiarly attractive," wrote Cabot. "The people are lords over their fine country, asking little favor, ever, save that the deer [caribou] may come in their time." They knew how to be happy even in adversity. In 1922, Rasmussen visited a Netsilingmiut fishing camp on King William Island. It was cold and the char had not yet come. "Ayornamat," shrugged the Eskimos, it can't be helped. The char were bound to come and in the meantime they danced and played, joyous and exuberant, as if they didn't have a care in the world. Rasmussen was deeply impressed: "Never in my life have I seen such frolicsome and happy people, so gaily starving, so cheerfully freezing in miserable ragged clothing." An Eskimo, said Stefansson, "laughs as much in a month as the average white man does in a year."

They loved to travel, enjoyed the change that each day brought, the small adventures of the trip, the anticipation of finding game. Their land, so drear and desolate at times, could, at other times, be rich and beautiful. Near the Ellice River in the 1930s, the Oblate priest Raymond de Coccola was travelling with Eskimos, when suddenly they came upon a vast herd of caribou, "a sight I shall never forget. Through a delicate haze that rose from the snow-covered land under the warm rays of the sun, caribou were visible everywhere. They were flowing from every gully, pass, and ravine, fanning out into the broad valley, pausing to graze, then slowly pushing on toward the glittering island-studded sea." And Diamond Jenness, travelling far across Victoria Island with an Eskimo family during its summer migration, gloried in the beauty of the land and the freedom of their life: "The earth was awakening to life again after its long sleep. Ducks and loons flew overhead, the ptarmigan in the valley were seeking out their mates, and a faint tinge of green had crept into the brown tips of the low dwarf willow that protruded above the snow. In the hills lay countless lakes teeming with trout and salmon, and herds of caribou grazed on the slopes and plains...food was abundant everywhere, so that we could roam where we pleased, as free and unfettered as the caribou we hunted."

Hunting was the men's work. But they did not think of it as such. For most it was a passion, a constant challenge. They hunted to live and they lived to hunt, and when a hunt was done, they re-lived it again at night, for all wanted to hear about it. It was a subject of never-ending fascination. As boys they had listened eagerly to the hunting tales of the men and had dreamt of the day when they too would return with seal or caribou to grateful and admiring relatives, who would rush from tents or huts to welcome the returning hunters:

"Joyfully
Greet we those
Who brought us plenty."

And when they were old, they recalled with nostalgia the hunting days of their youth, the far-flung travels, the joy of food:

"When one is no longer able to go hunting
How beautiful the mountains seem to be.
Brooks with their crystal clear water!
A roast on a fire of moss!
It is summer...the mosquitoes are gone!
One is happy to live!"

Theirs was in many ways a simple life with very basic joys: the joy of food, the joy of warmth, the joys of dancing and of story-telling, the joy of a sociable people in being together, the joy in children. "All the love of an Eskimo's nature centres on the children," wrote the Finnish geographer Vaino Tanner after spending more than a year with the people of Labrador. "One of the things an Eskimo loves most seems to be to make little children happy."

Hardship and happiness, these were the twin themes of the Eskimos' existence. Yet when they reminisce, it is usually the happiness they recall most vividly. Said Pitseolak, the Cape Dorset artist: "I had a happy childhood. I was always healthy and never sick...We lived in the old Eskimo way. We would pick up and go to different camps—we were free to move anywhere..."

And Ekalun of Bathurst Inlet told me once: "When I was young, we hunted very hard. We travelled much. If one was lucky, one had lots to eat. If one had no luck one was hungry. Often one was hungry. But then came again good times. And the people were happy and danced."

In 1977, the Canadian journalist Dorothy Eber went to Cape Dorset on Baffin Island with a set of very special photographs: portraits of Eskimos from this region taken in 1913-1914 by Robert Flaherty, who later became famous for his film *Nanook of the North*. The older people had a fine time recognizing relatives and friends of long ago. The younger were fascinated by these faces from another age. "They look so sure of themselves," said the 25-year-old Eskimo teacher Annie Manning. "They lived in their own culture."

A tired little girl is carried homewards pickaback by one of her companions.

A plane has come to an Eskimo camp in the central Canadian Arctic to take the school-age children to a far-away boarding school. The mother and small children watch them depart.

Her girl in her "amaut," an Eskimo woman shops at the supermarket in her arctic settlement.

Following page:
Wife and son watch as an Eskimo hunter skins a wolf he has shot.

A little Eskimo girl carries a hefty baby sister in the "amaut" of her woman's dress.

The Way of Life at an Arctic Camp

It was late in the evening when I returned from a walk inland to our camp near the coast of Arctic Sound. The storms of the preceding days had sculptured the snow into elongated drifts, each one ending in an elegant, slightly curved projection, like stylized birds frozen in flight. It was utterly still and very cold. The snow-covered land merged with the frozen sea and stretched out toward the horizon, infinite and empty. An arctic fox yapped querulously, spotted me and stopped, then trotted off on dainty, heavily-furred feet and vanished, a white wraith melting into the velvety-blue of the arctic night. Ahead four orange dots glowed faintly in the dark, four tents, four specks of life in this vast solitude, deathlike in its frozen stillness.

The sled dogs slept, dark lumps upon the bluish snow, tightly curled, noses tucked under bushy tails. I opened the door and ducked into "my" tent. Dwarf willow sputtered and crackled in the stove made out of a ten-gallon drum. Rosie was boiling seal meat in a huge pot. Clouds of steam rose from it, turned to milky vapor and to snow crystals upon the chill walls of the tent. The pressure lamp hissed; the crystal-lined tent glittered in its light. A raised sleeping platform of snow occupied half the tent. It was covered with a layer of caribou skins, fur side down, and two more layers fur side up. At the end of the platform lay our bedrolls and sacks with spare clothing. On the right-hand side of the tent was a low snow bench, covered with furs. The left-hand side was Rosie's domain. It contained the stove, a box that served both as table and as container for 20 enameled mugs, ours and spare ones for visitors, and shelves that held a radio, an alarm clock, tool boxes, skin scrapers, a Bible, and several tobacco cans full of needles, thimbles, knives, cigarette holders, pieces of bone and ivory, lumps of native cop-per, awls and various other tools and treasures, including a beautifully polished piece of jade that had presumably been obtained, ages ago, by barter from group to group all the way from Alaska. This was the home of Ekalun and his wife Rosie, and for three weeks it had been also my home.

I had come by dog team from Cambridge Bay on Victoria Island, an eight-day trip, and had arrived uninvited, unannounced and more than slightly apprehensive. It had seemed to me exceedingly presumptuous to arrive like that and ask to stay for half a year. Yet Ekalun had quietly agreed, had cleared a space six feet by three on the sleeping platform and that was now my realm. Whatever I left lying there, notebooks, or clothes, or camera equipment was quite inviolate. They did not ask me whence I came, nor why, nor who I was. I shared their food, I shared their tents, I was a part of their lives, and yet apart. To pry into my life and motives would have been a breach of courtesy, an invasion of my freedom as an individual to divulge information or withhold it. Often in the months to come, I was guiltily aware how poorly my inquisitiveness compared to their polite restraint. Only rarely, and then usually obliquely, would Ekalun let me know that he considered me a nosy nuisance. He had been about ten years old when he saw his first white men, members of Stefansson's expedition. "What were they like these first white men you met?" I asked, curiously. "Just like you, Kabloo," he shot back. "Forever asking questions."

The meat was ready. Rosie fished out the chunks with a pointed stick, placed them on a large, oval, wooden platter, then added seal blood to the broth, stirring vigorously to prevent the blood from clotting. She opened the door and called "Seal's ready!" and after a while the other members of the camp came over: George, Ekalun's son, Jessie, his beautiful wife, and two children, a baby, a little lump on Jessie's back beneath her voluminous fur cloak, and Karetak, two years old, dark-eyed and droll, the pampered pet of the clan; Moses, another son, and his wife Ella, with four children, a baby, Papak, a seven-year-old boy, quiet and pleasant, Puglik, five, and her little brother Oched, a strong-willed, energetic three-year-old, whose natural tendency to rambunctiousness was gently dampened by the adults; and Mary, Ekalun's daughter, with Kaneak, her husband, and their five-year-old daughter. It seemed incredible that so many people, most dressed in bulky furs, could fit into our little tent. Yet all found space to sit or squat, each took a chunk of steaming meat, bit into it and sliced off a bite-sized piece with a razor-sharp knife, the blade just missing nose and lips. All had blood soup and partially filled cups stood everywhere, yet none was spilled. Jessie cut little pieces of meat for Karetak, but Oched already wielded a knife. At first he grabbed a skinning knife, its keen-edged blade and oil-slippery handle nearly as long as his arm. No one objected. But when, as was to be expected, he nicked his thumb, he got no sympathy. All laughed, a bit derisively. Ella picked up the knife he had dropped, gave him another, less long and lethal, and Oched, fighting back the tears of pain, continued the meal with more caution, sucking his bleeding thumb from time to time.

The meal, like all our meals, was quietly relaxed. Moses had been hunting all day. He was hungry and ate a lot, a sheen of perspiration spreading across his darkly handsome face. The others had eaten before; for some it was the fourth or fifth meal of the day. They ate a bit, wiped off their hands on one of the ptarmigan skins that served as towels, poured tea, added lots of sugar, reached for Ekalun's tobacco can, rolled cigarettes and smoked. The children, full of meat, were drowsy. They fell asleep right where they sat, lolling against the

adults. Moses told about his hunt. He started slowly, diffidently, addressing no one in particular. He told of the trip, of the wolf tracks he had seen, of waiting long for a seal to surface in its "agloo," the breathing hole beneath the snow. The others listened, absorbed in every facet of the tale. Finally the seal had come. He had driven the harpoon down through the snow with all his force, but a chip of ice deflected it and the seal had escaped. There was a chorus of commiserating "ahs." Moses had been out for 14 hours in that bitter cold and had returned with nothing. "Ayornamat," it can't be helped.

Then it was my turn. Haltingly, in very simple and execrable Eskimo, I told of my walk, of the things I had seen, of the animal tracks I had followed. They listened with exemplary patience. They rarely laughed about my efforts and often lauded them. Only later, as I became more familiar with their life, did I realize that in many ways they were treating me as they would treat children. Whenever I helped with any work and did it reasonably well, they were quick and generous in their praise. And when we had visitors, Eskimos from other camps, they would relate in my presence my positive achievements, so I could bask in everyone's approval. Minor foibles and transgressions were curbed by teasing and by expert satiric mimicking of my displeasing traits. Serious offences against approved behavior were punished by a withdrawal of affection. This was very subtle, very unpleasant and extremely effective.

My most grievous sin was impulsive assertiveness. After being imprisoned by storms for a week, chafing at the inactivity, I awoke one morning to find the weather perfect and Ekalun all set to leave. "Where to?" I asked. "To a far-away island to get soapstone," he said. I knew there were ancient house ruins that I very much wanted to see on that island. "I'm coming along," I said. He muttered something about the dogs being weak and the ice bad, a veiled warning I should have heeded. But I desperately wanted to go and felt that, as a paying border, I had a certain right to come along. So I insisted. Ekalun turned abruptly, unharnessed the dogs, went back to his tent and began to work on a carving.

By their cultural tenets, I had committed a grave offence. I had curtailed his freedom. Everyone in camp did just as he pleased. If someone felt like leaving, he left; if he felt like sleeping, he slept; if he felt like carving, he carved. If I spent hours trying to dig out lemmings to take their pictures, that was my affair. They might regard it as silly and futile, but it was a harmless activity that interfered with no one else. By my impetuous demand to be taken along, I had broken the basic rule of non-interference in other people's plans or actions.

For the next eight days I lived miserably under a chilly cloud of general disapproval. There was nothing tangible about it. I still shared their tents and their food, but I no longer shared in the human warmth of camp life. The gentle friendly harmony was gone. The "we" had broken into "they" and "I," and they were in and I was out. It was amazing how drastically this affected me. I became moody and morose. In my increasingly neurotic state it seemed to me that even the children were avoiding me. I was filled with baffled anger that changed to sulky self-reproach. I went for endless lonely walks. On the eighth day I

returned late, glum and famished. Rosie had just called her "Seal's ready!" and all were in her tent. I squeezed in and squatted near the door. The quiet of our meal, so pleasantly relaxed before, now seemed ominously tense and brooding. I ate quickly, nervously. It gave me something to do. Suddenly Ekalun looked up and smiled. "You walk all day alone, like amarok, the wolf. And now you eat just like a wolf." I recognized that tone of voice. It was the gentle banter of before. I laughed and then the others laughed, and our common laughter lifted the icy cloud from me and it vanished in a wave of friendly warmth. I once again belonged. I was deeply happy and content, and henceforth took the greatest care to curb my assertiveness so I would not offend again.

Thus, slowly, sometimes painfully, by prod and praise, and various subtle sanctions and rewards, they modified my behavior to conform more closely to their culturally accepted norms. It also made me understand why the children at our camp were so well-behaved. At first it had seemed to me that the attitude of the adults toward the children was one of total laissez-faire. The children were never beaten, never scolded. Not once in more than six months did I hear an adult yell at a child. The children appeared free to do whatever they liked, whenever they liked. They often slept half the day, then played far into the night. They came to meals, or stayed away, helping themselves to the always available food whenever they were hungry. Despite this permissiveness, they were pleasant, peaceful, rarely got into mischief, were eager to assist, to take on little chores, and played with each other, endlessly, with virtually no fuss or fighting. With them the gradual, infinitely patient process of conditioning had already begun when they were babies.

There were two babies at our camp. Jessie's had just been born. Ella's was three months old. At night it slept next to her, close against her body. In daytime it lived in her "amaut," the pouch-like enlargement of her voluminous fur cloak, always in close, reassuring contact with its mother. It only had to peep and she shifted it beneath her cloak from back to front to let it nurse. Most of the time it seemed to sleep, warm and secure in its pouch, and sometimes one could hear it mew and mumble there, like a contented kitten. But even the warmest babies have their whims and moods, and occasionally it rebelled, squirming and kicking. Ella ignored it for a while, or jiggled rhythmically to lull the baby back to sleep. When that did not help, she stiffened her body. That was the baby's cue to settle down. If it ignored this warning, she sometimes pulled it out, all naked except for a diaper, and placed it upon the sleeping platform. There it lay in the chilly air, like a frantic beetle on its back, waving arms and legs and screaming furiously. She never left it long. She picked it up, cuddled it, shushed it, showered it with love and endearments and, when it was quiet again and happy, she popped it into its cozy nest upon her back. The baby quickly learned that the tensing of its mother's body meant annoyance, a warning of possible separation, and usually responded promptly to such subtle signals.

Both babies lived in an aura of love, not just their mothers' love but in the effusive affection of everyone in camp. When Moses came back from hunting, he often played with the baby. He bounced it softly on his knees, his powerful dark hands encompassing its plump little body, and crooned songs for it. Oched and Puglik were encouraged to play with the baby, though Ella kept a careful eye on Oched.

Puglik was gentle and affectionate with the baby (her mother had made her a rag doll which she now often carried in the back of her parka). But Oched was a tempestuous little boy who got easily carried away. He either poked the baby with a grubby finger, or smothered it with so much love, the poor thing could barely breathe, and Ella gently intervened.

Karetak was the pride and pet of everyone in camp. He was our little clown, the pampered darling of all. Whenever he was there, he was the center of affection and attention. All this should have turned him into an insufferable brat, but he really was a very nice child, full of radiant happiness, always pert though sometimes pesky. He was just beginning to speak. After a meal, someone would say a phrase for Karetak and he repeated it, mimicking the intonation and the gestures of the adult. Soon it became a good-natured, happy game. Karetak, his eyes shining with pleasure at being the focus of attention, would parody us all. They egged him on: "How does the white man eat his meat?" and Karetak pretended to bite into a chunk of meat, look at it in cross-eyed concentration and cut it very gingerly. It was amusing and never mean. Everyone laughed and Karetak, delighted with his success, would imitate someone else.

He needed love and attention. Until recently his mother had nursed him and he had spent much time in her amaut, snuggled against her body. Now the baby had displaced him.

For a while he still asked to be carried and since this was now impossible for Jessie, she sent him to our tent and Rosie took him on her back, her small, work-worn body bent beneath his weight. At the same time, he was gently teased by everyone about his wish to be in the amaut and as the weather grew warmer, he played increasingly outside and did not ask any more to be carried. But he did miss being nursed. In their tent, Jessie would let him nurse occasionally. But when he asked for it while other adults were present, they chaffed him and offered him instead choice bits of meat, bannock with jam, or some other delicacy. The general policy was never to deny him a wish or frustrate a desire, but to distract him with lots of love and affection, and then offer him a substitute.

Once, in their tent, Jessie was sitting on the sleeping platform sewing a wolverine ruff for a parka hood. Karetak took a piece of the valuable fur and, playing with his mother's scissors, began to clip the hairs. Jessie rummaged in a bag and pulled out a piece of worthless caribou skin. She played with Karetak for a while, then showed him how to use the scissors properly, deftly substituting caribou fur for wolverine, and both continued with their "work."

The baby wriggled in the amaut. Jessie extracted it and changed its diaper, while Karetak watched with fond curiosity. The baby fascinated him but although it had replaced him in the amaut, he did not appear to be jealous. Whenever George and Jessie played with the baby and fussed over it, they always included Karetak, encouraging him to gently pet and kiss the baby, all sharing in a common love. Karetak at the age of two could do no wrong and actually he rarely did. That baffled me at first. But then I realized that the near-total indulgence he enjoyed was balanced by a very subtle, patient process of persuasion. If he was nice and pleasant and well-behaved, everyone in camp showered him with lavish praise. His smallest accomplishment, like putting boots on by himself, was commented upon. But if he misbehaved, he was gently

teased and coaxed, and the general warmth and affection that normally enveloped him decreased perceptibly.

With Oched, three years old, this pushing in the desired behavioral direction, was already a bit less subtle and velvety. His demands no longer elicited an immediate and indulgent response. That angered him. He screamed in fury and pummeled his mother with his fists. She did not fend him off; he was too small to hurt her. She merely laughed. And if others were present they, too, would laugh, and this was mocking laughter. The more he raged, the more derisive the laughter became, until he ceased and subsided in a flood of impotent tears. Only then would Ella pick him up and cuddle him. Since such fits of temper rarely achieved anything except to expose him to ridicule, he slowly became less demanding, less assertive and more self-reliant.

Ours was a timeless life. There were clocks in every tent and most adults wore wrist watches, but the time they showed was really of no concern, for all did as we pleased. Weather, mood and need were the determinatives of our existence. Time as measured by our watches existed on a different plane, as an abstract entity that we ignored. Rosie was usually the first to rise. She dressed quickly for the tent was icy, lit the stove and put the kettle on. As it got warm, Ekalun got up and then, sleepy and a bit reluctant, I would emerge from my sleeping bag and get dressed. Rosie called "Tea's ready!" and after a while some of the other adults would appear to drink tea and eat meat or bannock. The children, as a rule, were still asleep in their respective tents. Ella ate and left, the others chatted and smoked. Then Ella called and we went to her tent for a second breakfast and later, perhaps, to Mary's for a third. If the weather was good, the men usually left to hunt seal. They would be gone for ten to fifteen hours. The women sewed, repaired clothing, played with the children, scraped skins or visited each other. The children slept. Toward noon, Papak crept out from underneath the furs on the sleeping platform, drank lukewarm tea and ate some meat, dressed and went out to play. Puglik soon followed him. Oched slept on. But when he woke and found the others gone, he was in a tearing hurry to be out and join them. While Ella watched, fondly amused, he struggled into parka, pants and boots. It would have gone much faster had she helped him, but the tendency was to encourage children to do things by themselves. She did tie his sealskin boots properly and was about to tie on his caribou mitts, but Oched, ajitter with impatience, just couldn't wait. He squirmed away and dashed out of the tent, leaving the mitts behind. Ella calmly continued with her sewing. It was ten below outside so, not surprisingly, Oched was back in a few minutes, blowing urgently into bright-red fists. Ella laughed a bit and petted him, warmed his hands upon her warm body, tied on the mitts and he was off again.

Except in severe storms, the children played outside all day and far into the night. They also worked. Not because anyone asked them to but because they liked to do it. It gave them a sense of importance and this was fostered by approving comments from all the adults. In spring a lead opened in the ice not far from camp and the children spent patient hours jigging for polar cod, then returned triumphantly with a handful or two of the little fish. One of the mothers cleaned them and boiled them for supper. It was an insipid, watery soup with lots of bones, but all dutifully enthused about this "delicious" meal. On the whole they were a happy, busy little tribe, but I did feel sorry for Papak. He was a quiet, pleasant boy, less boisterous than Oched, but always ready to play with the smaller children, patient and good-natured. Occasionally he went off on his own. Moses had made him a bow and arrows, and in spring he stalked snow buntings and sandpipers with great determination but little success. At times he seemed pensive and withdrawn. Once, in early summer, as I came back from a walk, I saw him sitting alone on a ridge a mile from camp. The ground was soft and he did not hear me until I was directly behind him. He glanced up, startled, and I could see he had been crying. He quickly turned away and I walked on, pretending not to notice. This was his last year at the camp. In the fall the plane would come and take him to a boarding school in a northern town. He had never been away before, spoke only Eskimo and I wondered in pity if it was fear of that far-away alien world that had driven him to cry alone on the ridge above our camp.

An Endless Source of Joy

The men from our camp at Arctic Sound left early to hunt seals. It was one of those rare enchanted days in early spring when the Arctic is sublime: the sky a clear robin-egg blue turning to cool green near the horizon, the snow brilliantly aglitter, the air as fresh and pure as chilled champagne. Evaporation haze danced and flickered above the ridges beyond our camp. The dogs ran happy, eagerly, tails cockily curled over their backs, and the long, pliant sleds undulated smoothly across the waves of drifted, hard-packed snow.

It took three hours to reach the sealing grounds, a vast expanse of snow-covered ice. In fall each ringed seal scrapes holes through the forming ice, and keeps these "agloos" open as vital vents to the air above. The men used their dogs to sniff out the breathing holes beneath the snow, then inserted "idlaks," thin slivers of wood with colored tassels on their tops, through the snow into the agloo below. When a seal comes up to breathe, the idlak jiggles and the hunter plunges his harpoon through the snow into the seal. Each man spread a piece of thick caribou fur on the snow to muffle even the slightest noise from his feet and froze into immobility, bent over like a three-quarter-closed jack-knife, his eyes riveted to the tiny, colored tassel of the idlak, his harpoon held at the ready. The morning passed. The men stood motionless, dark, silent shapes upon the blinding white. Each seal has many breathing holes. It may be hours, it can be days, before he surfaces in the one where the hunter waits. "I have heard of a man who spent two-and-a-half days at a breathing hole..." Rasmussen once wrote. The wind picked up and instantly it became intensely cold. Snow swirled and raced across the ice. The men stood still as statues, their entire being concentrated upon that minute speck of color at the top of each idlak. Midafternoon. They had not budged. Suddenly Moses straightened, lifted his harpoon high and with one smooth, immensely powerful motion drove it into the surfacing seal. He held the harpoon line with one hand, cut away snow and ice with his long knife, killed the seal and hauled it out onto the ice. He sat and smoked, his back turned to the cutting wind, then fetched the dogs to search for another agloo.

Night came, the wind increased in strength. The hunting day was finished. Moses had his seal; for the other three men the long, icy vigil had been in vain. The sun set, a baleful, chilly, orange orb; snow flurries danced, golden in its slanting rays. The huskies were cold and raced toward home. The men sat humped upon the sleds, tired now and drained after so many hours of total concentration, and we travelled into the night, a phantom procession of dogs and sleds rushing silently through the gloom and drifting snow.

Despite the cold and wind, women and children dashed out to greet us, helped to unharness and tether the dogs. It felt warm in the tents; the tea was boiling. We shook the snow out of our furs and sat in grateful silence. We drank the sweet, hot tea, mug after mug, and a sensuous glow spread through our stiff, chilled bodies. The women cut up the seal, each taking a portion, for all the food was shared. We ate from tent to tent, starting with a huge meal at Ella's. It was past midnight when we went to Mary's tent to eat some tidbits, drink more tea, smoke and sit together, sated and relaxed, talking about the hunt, the children, the small incidents of the day. Mary looked tired. A pile of scraped skins showed she had worked hard all day. Her kind, narrow face was drawn and haggard. We dawdled deliciously, tired and content. It was past 1 a.m. when we finally went to bed.

At breakfast next day, Mary still appeared to be tired. I heard an odd little mewing sound. "What's that?" I asked.

"The baby," Mary said.

"Whose baby?"

"My baby," Mary smiled.

"When was it born?" I asked, amazed. With all those voluminous fur clothes I hadn't even realized Mary had been pregnant.

"Oh, last night after supper," Mary said, and went out to shovel away snow that had drifted against the tent during the night. Six days later she and her husband left for a long hunting trip inland.

Eskimo women in former days, said Peter Freuchen, referred to giving birth as a mere inconvenience. His own wife, Navarana, bore a child at 3 a.m., got up at 8 a.m. to "straighten her house" and then went for a walk with the baby. That evening, to celebrate the occasion, they held a grand party and Navarana "danced with abandon" most of the night. When Henry Larsen, captain of the RCMP ship *St. Roch* attended Easter mass at Pelly Bay in 1942, a young Eskimo woman fainted in the crowded church. He helped her out, she quickly recovered, smiled her thanks and went back into the church. "Afterwards I learned that she had just come about one hundred miles and had given birth to a baby a few hours before the service." At Point Hope in Alaska in the 1950s, the artist Claire Fejes saw an Eskimo woman go down to the beach to cut up whale meat. She was interrupted in her work by the birth of her child and returned after a while to the village "carrying her baby." If a child was born during a trip, a common occurrence among a people who formerly travelled much, it was customary to set up a tent or build an ingloo where the woman could give birth, to let her rest for a few hours and then continue.

The mother knelt while giving birth, in some groups alone, secluded in a special tent or igloo, in others assisted by a midwife. She wiped the baby clean with ground squirrel skins, if it was a girl, so it would grow up to be as quick and lovely as a squirrel, or, if it was a boy, with the skin from the forehead of a caribou bull, so he would grow into a mighty and successful hunter of caribou.

In some groups, the baby was carried naked in the amaut, in others it wore a little diaper of caribou fur. Eskimo mothers on southern Baffin Island, noted Franz Boas in the late 19th century, made caps of down-soft hare fur for their babies and shirts and booties of fawn skin. Tied to these tiny garments in the past were often amulets, to imbue the baby with their magic and aid it in the future: a raven's foot, for the raven is hardy and shrewd; bone from a wolf, to be as fast and enduring as the wolf; a tuft of fox fur, to be as agile as a fox; an ermine's tail, to be a hunter as lithe and skillfull as the ermine; a ptarmigan's leg, to blend with the land like this cryptically-colored bird.

To have children was everyone's greatest wish and they were deeply loved. "All [Eskimos]... love children," noted the biologist Sally Carrighar in Alaska, and among the Netsilingmiut of the central Canadian Arctic the ethnologist Asen Balikci found "...children at all ages were an endless source of joy to their parents." Eskimos at Chantrey Inlet told Jean Briggs that the first-born is often especially loved because its parents have looked "forward so much to having children." If children failed to come, Eskimo women in some regions ate large quantities of seaweed in the belief that this would stimulate fertility. "Piaraliksak" was the name given to certain seaweeds along Hudson Strait, '(the plant) that promotes the potential for there being a baby.' Until missionaries told them otherwise, Eskimos saw no sin or shame in a child being born to an unmarried woman. The notion of "illegitimacy" was alien to them, their language lacks the word. The girl was free to keep the child or to offer it for adoption. If she kept it, it was no hindrance to her marital

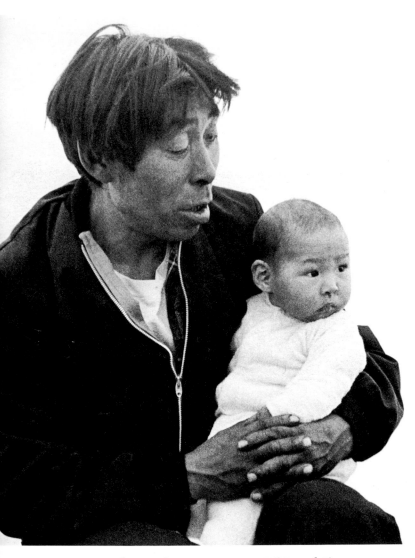

Home from a hunting trip, an Eskimo father croons a song for his baby.

A little Eskimo girl shares a tidbit with her father.

A tired Lapp woman holds her child who is fascinated by the flickering flames of the camp fire.

An Eskimo woman feeds small pieces of boiled caribou meat to her baby.

Following page:
In Greenland, the father has shot a seal; his son hauls it away from the edge of rotting ice to their sled left on thicker ice.

Their father's reindeer lasso tied to a sloping tree near camp makes a swing for Lapp children in early summer.

Opposite:
On a fall evening at low tide, Polar Eskimo children in Greenland play on the glistening rocks near shore.

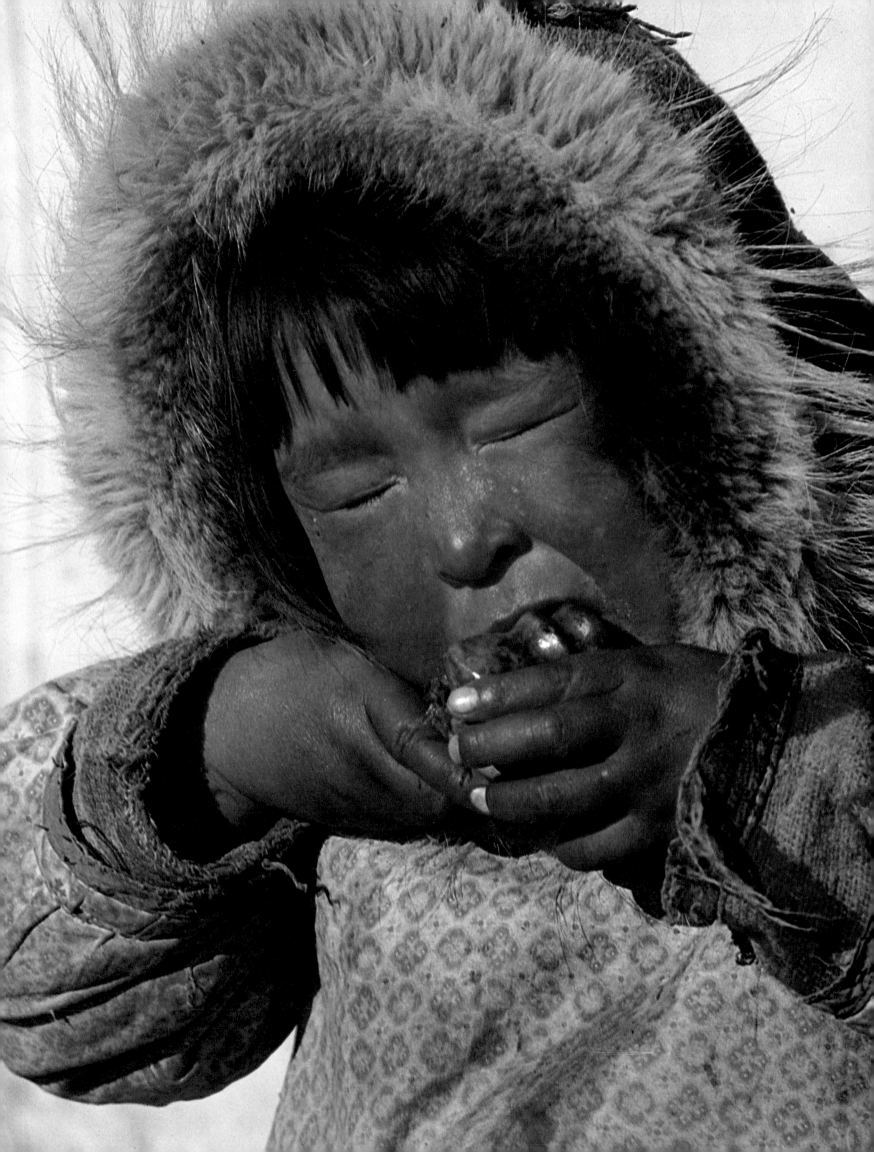

Caribou marrow, raw or boiled, is a favorite delicacy.

A berry picker on Hudson Strait gives a sprig of crowberries to her child in the "amaut."

Eskimo family cleaning whitefish; some help, some prefer to watch.

A little girl tries to get the marrow out of a bone.

Helped by his wife and son, a Polar Eskimo in northwest Greenland cuts up a white whale.

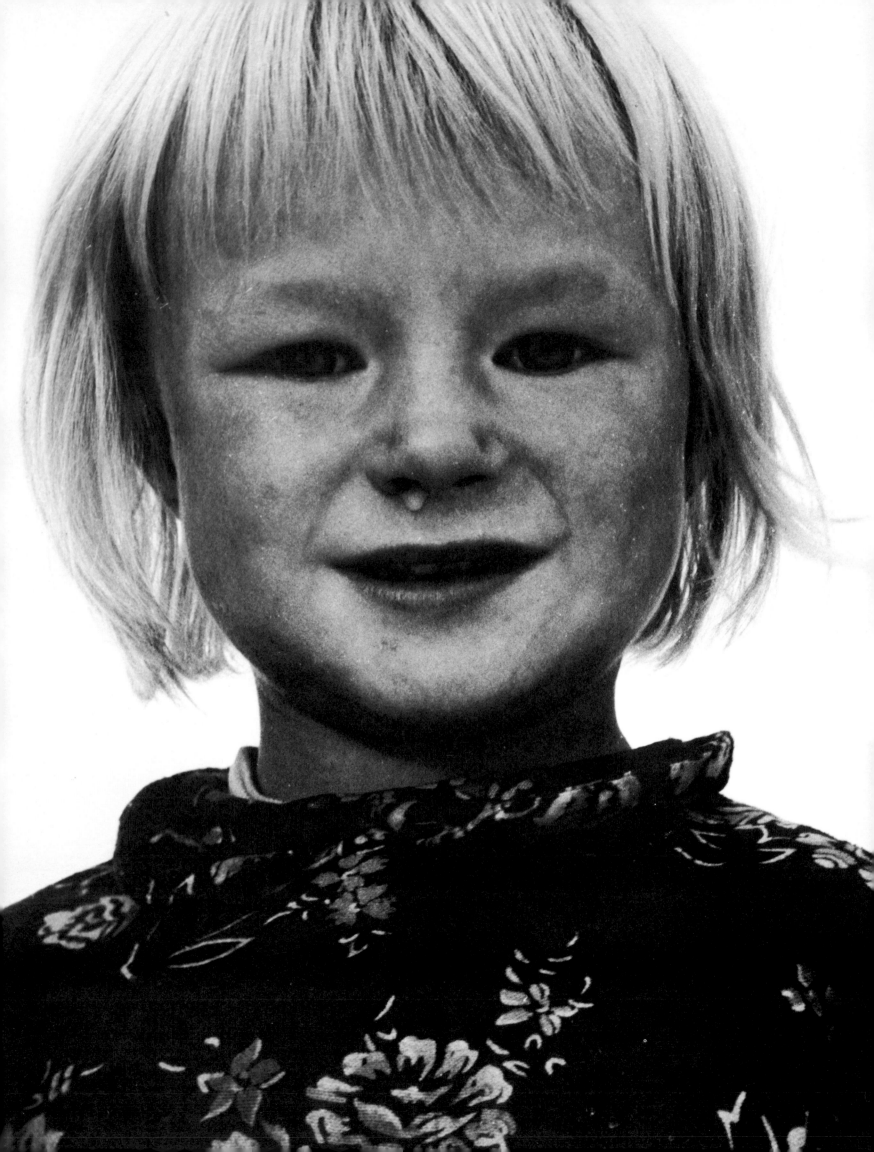

Opposite:
A reflective Eskimo girl on a bus
in a northern settlement.

A pensive Eskimo girl, all dressed to play outside, waits patiently for
a friend to get ready and join her.

Preceding page:
Indian children play at a forest
lake in northernmost Manitoba.

83

In fall on Baffin Island, an Eskimo girl collects berries.

*An Eskimo girl works on her
composition in a school at
Repulse Bay in the eastern
Canadian Arctic.*

prospects. In former days it even enhanced them, especially if it was a boy, and her husband would raise and love the child precisely as if it was his own.

Despite this intense love for children, some Eskimo groups in the past practiced infanticide. This was the dictate not of a cruel people but of a harsh and grudging land. Infanticide was rare among the people of such game-rich regions as coastal Alaska, Labrador and Greenland, and most prevalent among the Netsilingmiut and other groups of the central Canadian Arctic where game was often scarce and people were haunted by the fear of famine.

A Netsilik hunter told Rasmussen: "Life is so with us that we are never surprised when we hear that someone has starved to death. We are so used to it. It sometimes happens to the best of us." And when Rasmussen remarked that the people appeared joyous and content, one man exclaimed: "Oh! You strangers only see us happy and free of care. But if you knew the horrors we often have to live through, you would understand too why we are so fond of laughing, why we love food and song and dancing. There is not one among us but has experienced a winter of bad hunting, when many people starved to death around us and when we ourselves pulled through only by accident."

In this grim struggle for survival, it was the hunting skill of the men which decided the fate of all. Therefore boys were ardently desired as future hunters and providers, while girls were regarded as a drain upon the meager food resources. Since most Eskimo women nursed their children for two to three years and sometimes longer and during this time rarely conceived, children normally were born at three to four-year intervals. By eliminating female babies at birth, the chances for having boys were considerably enhanced. Rasmussen met a Netsilik couple who had had 20 children. Ten girls had been killed at birth, four had died of disease and one boy had perished

in a kayak accident. Five children remained, four boys and a girl, all "handsome and powerful Eskimos." When Rasmussen asked whether the couple did not regret having killed so many girls, they said "no, for without killing she would not have had so many children, and if she had had to suckle all the girls, who were born before the boys, she would have had no sons now." The child was killed immediately after birth, "before the parents grow attached to it," and invariably before it had received a name. Once named, its life was sacred and inviolate.

The name, most people of the north believed, was closely allied with a person's soul, had, in fact, a soul or spirit of its own. When a person died it was thought that its name-soul (some groups believed in a plurality of souls) lingered on in the vicinity, waiting patiently. Afterwards when a child was born it was given the dead person's name and the name-spirit became its guardian, guiding it through its formative years. As a child's own soul and spirit developed and its individuality increased, the strength and influence of its guardian soul waned and eventually it vanished. Since children were named after relatives who had been loved and revered, a part of them fused with each coming generation. "It is only the names of the wicked that are blotted out forever," noted the Oblate missionary Arsène Turquetil. Thus while the evil were expunged in body, soul and name and simply ceased to be, the good lived on in name and soul and memory, each one the guardian of a child. This belief was in part responsible for the fact that northern children were never beaten and rarely scolded, for to do so would have been a grave affront to their respective guardian spirits.

Since children, as a rule, were so very much desired and so deeply loved, couples who had none or few were anxious to adopt them. This love of children and compassion for them are enduring traits.

One Sunday in an arctic village where I lived,

the priest, trying to make the point that not all whites are affluent and free of care, spoke movingly about the plight of southern slum children: of poor housing, bad and insufficient food, foul city air, of children playing on grimy streets. The next day an Eskimo woman came to see him. "You know, Father," she said, "my husband and I had a long talk last night and we've decided to adopt a few of those poor white kids." The priest, though touched, and gratified at the impact of his sermon, did his best to dissuade her, for she already had 14 children of her own.

On Baffin Island in the 1880s Franz Boas noted that adoptions were very common. "If for any reason a man is unable to provide for his family or if a woman cannot do her household work, the children are adopted by a relative or a friend, who considers them as his own children." At about the same time, three thousand miles to the west, the naturalist John Murdoch observed: "The custom of adoption is universal at Point Barrow" and such children were raised by their adoptive parents with all the love and affection given to their own children. "...women who have several children frequently give away one or more of them...we know of one case where a woman who had lost a young infant had another given to her by one of her friends."

Adoption was never surrounded by secrecy. As the adopted child grew up it was told who its natural parents were, but its loyalty and love remained, as a rule, centred upon its adoptive parents. If adoption took place among close kin, relationships, at least to an outsider, could be confusing. I once lived at a camp in the western Arctic where an elderly couple had adopted one of their son's children. The boy now referred to his grandparents as "mother and father," to his natural father as "my brother" and to his mother as "my sister-in-law," while to his real brothers and sisters he was "our uncle," although they were older than he.

Thus every child was wanted and no child

lacked a loving home except, oddly enough, the orphan. The neglected, maltreated orphan is a recurrent theme in Eskimo legends and tales. Often he lives with his grandmother and they make a pathetic, appealing pair: the worn old woman, rheumy and bent, and the slender, eager child, both dressed in rags, both hungry, living on scraps in a tattered tent that is forever cold. Ranged against them are the other villagers, mean people, fat, avaricious, arrogant. They never share with the poor and often they maltreat them. Only one or two families show compassion and sometimes give them food and castoff clothing. Then, in pity, the spirits intervene. The moon spirit, who is the protector of orphans, or the bear spirit, infuse the orphan with some of their might. The next time one of the cruel villagers knocks him about, the boy beats him to pulp and then slays all the others, sparing only those who were kind to him and his grandmother. There are hundreds of variants of this tale, but the basic theme is always the same: the poor, mistreated orphan becomes a mighty man and kills his erstwhile tormentors who denied him food, shelter and love when he was a child.

Apart from being tales with an obvious moral, they contained a considerable amount of truth. In Greenland, long ago, especially among the otherwise kind and extremely generous Polar Eskimos, orphans led a miserable existence. Freuchen tells of one, Qupagnuk (the Snow Bunting), who "had to forage for himself," wore ragged, worn-out garments discarded by the adults and slept in the entrance tunnels of abandoned houses. When the men fed their sled dogs, Qupagnuk came running, "jumped in among the voracious, battling dogs, who often bit him in the face and on the hands," and wolfed down scraps of meat. When Freuchen reproached the men for such cruelty and neglect, they said: "An orphan who has a hard time should never be pitied, for he is merely being hardened for a better life. Look, and you will see that the greatest...hunters living here have all been orphans." But there the similarity with the legends ends. Far from revenging themselves on their oppressors, these real-life orphans grown into mighty hunters were usually famous for their kindness and hospitality. The same was true on Baffin Island where, Peter Pitseolak of Cape Dorset said that the poorest boys often grew into the best men. "I think these people who had hard times when they were young, try to be kind to poor people. They know what it's all about."

Nuligak, an Eskimo from the western Arctic, born near the end of the last century, was an orphan and "really knew what misery meant." He lived with his grandmother who was partly paralyzed. She cooked, and repaired his clothes which were "little more than rags ...How I have envied children who were not poor!" Nuligak hunted. He had no gun, but he made snares and caught ground squirrels, ducks and geese. "...two geese was the biggest weight I could carry. I was only 10 years old." It was hard. "It is not funny...to be a self-supporting little orphan — everything frightened me."

At the age of eleven, he obtained two traps. He captured foxes and sold their pelts. He bought a gun, two dogs and a sled. He travelled widely, the little boy leading his dogs, his crippled grandmother riding on the sled. When he was 13 he killed his first white whale. "I was very proud." In 1911, he was travelling with a group of people. His grandmother was very sick. His dogs, poorly fed, were weak. It was November, the days were short, the wind icy. The others hurried on. They were alone. Nuligak had just turned 16. "I was afraid...neither of us had anything to eat." They had no tent. His grandmother said: "Little one, don't stay here alone, go, follow the rest." And then she added, regretfully "And to think that I have not finished making your clothes yet." That night she died. The boy cried bitterly, in loneliness and desperation. She had been the only person he

had deeply loved. He put her body on the sled and thus they travelled on through the days and arctic nights, the hungry, lonely boy and his dead grandmother, until he reached the village of Tuktoyaktuk and there he buried her. Although his early life was extremely hard, some people were kind to him. He never forgot. Later he became a famous and fairly prosperous hunter and trapper and nothing gave him more pleasure than to provide with food those people who had helped him when he was a poor little orphan.

Most children, of course, grew up in the closeness and warmth of family life and, as a rule, were so pleasant that many early explorers were utterly charmed by them. Wrote William Edward Parry after meeting Eskimos in northern Foxe Basin in 1822: "The affection of parents for their children was frequently displayed... not only in the mere passive indulgence and abstinence from corporal punishment...but by a thousand playful endearments...Nothing, indeed, can well exceed the kindness with which they treat their children....the gentleness and docility of the children are such as to occasion their parents little trouble and to render severity towards them quite unnecessary. Even from their earliest infancy, they possess that quiet disposition, gentleness of demeanor, and uncommon evenness of temper, for which in more mature age they are for the most part distinguished. Disobedience is scarcely ever known; a word or even a look from a parent is enough; I never saw a single instance of that frowardness and disposition to mischief which, in our youth, so often requires the whole attention of a parent to watch over and correct. They never cry from trifling accidents, and sometimes not even from very severe hurts, at which an English child would sob for an hour..." (There is a certain wistfulness in this account due, perhaps, to the fact that Parry was 13 when he joined the Royal Navy, notorious for its ruthless discipline. Another explorer who wrote movingly about the kindness of Eskimo parents to their children was Parry's contemporary John Ross. He joined the Royal Navy at the age of nine.) With Eskimos the basis of raising children was lots of love, coupled with gentle guidance, endless patience, and a firm belief that the ultimate response to kindness, combined with unobtrusive but persistent coaxing, would be goodness. In Alaska an Eskimo woman told the biologist Sally Carrighar: "We talk to them every day about being nice. Children know what 'nice' is...they just know what goodness is. When they are born, they know. We keep reminding them when they forget." And a man recalled: "My parents talked to us at most of our meals and in the evening about being good people. As soon as the babies could understand, they were hearing these things, and so they were trained to be good before they were old enough to be bad."

An Eskimo hunter from Wales in Alaska explained to Miss Carrighar why Eskimos do not punish children. "Eskimo parents do not approve of striking a child, because then the child will feel ugly. He will want to strike someone himself. In our family we were encouraged to be good—not scolded. We could feel we were being loved, and that made us love right back."

An overt show of affection among adults, even among parents and older children, was frowned upon. The Polar Eskimos, said Freuchen, "resent public displays of emotion...and to express worry or concern over an absent mate is shocking." This was rooted in part in their strong feeling for individual freedom and independence. "An...adult [Eskimo] wants to be self-sufficient, and not a cause of concern or an object of pity to others," noted Jean Briggs, who lived for more than a year with an Eskimo family at a remote camp. But little children were effusively and exuberantly loved. "It is toward small children that the Utkuhikhalingmiut express affection...most openly, most completely. They are snuffed, cuddled, cooed at, talked to, and played with

endlessly, the men as demonstrative as the women." Jean Briggs' family had a little girl. In the evening, after the mother had tucked her in and was still busy with the last chores, the father talked to the girl, teaching her the names of their dogs, their relatives and various other words and names which she would "mimic...in her docile chirp." When she pronounced the words well, she was warmly praised by her parents. It was a gentle, happy lesson-game that was played each evening until "the pupil fell asleep." Then the father still spoke to her "his voice stroking her endearingly as she slept. It was baby talk he cooed... at her so gently; but the tone diffused a tenderness over all of us."

The artist Claire Fejes who lived with Eskimos in Alaska in the 1950s was also impressed by the gentle, happy tenor of camp life. "All the time I was in the camp, I never heard...any of the...women rebuke or say a harsh word to their children, nor did the children seem to fight with one another. There was a refreshing absence of nagging, yelling, and bullying between parent and child. Love seemed to surround these children from birth and to envelop them, love given not only by mother and father, aunt and uncle, but by everyone in camp."

Eskimos feared anger. Anger, they felt, led to more anger that might culminate in dangerous hostility and strife. An old Eskimo woman in Lake Harbour on southern Baffin Island told Archibald Fleming, later bishop of the Arctic, in 1914, "it was a grievous thing to raise one's voice, since that indicated anger and anger led to quarreling and to other evils."

The ideal person in their view was one who was even-tempered, tactful, generous, kind, quiet, happy and, above all, reasonable. Conversely, they loathed and feared people who were ill-tempered, tactless, avaricious, mean, loud, querulous and unreasonable. Such people were avoided, ridiculed in lampoon songs and, in extreme cases, ostracized.

Small children, the Eskimos felt, lacked "ihuma," reason. In the Eskimo view, noted Jean Briggs "growing up is largely a process of acquiring ihuma." Since the small child lacks reason, it was to be expected that its behavior should at times be unreasonable. Hence the anger and the temper, the fretting and the fussing of a small child were accepted and tolerated as being merely the outward symptoms of its lack of ihuma. "Because children are unreasoning beings, unable to understand that their distresses are illusory, people are at pains to reassure them," Jean Briggs wrote. They were pampered and petted, humored and, above all, lavishly loved, not only by their parents but by the whole camp community. The "initial socialization for Eskimo children is among the most lenient and positively supportive" among all human cultures, according to the Alaskan psychologist Arthur E. Hippler. "Such close intense relationships lead to the development of a generally secure and optimistic ego. The child becomes confident that the universe is essentially benign." But, as the teacher Margery Hinds observed in the 1960s at Arctic Bay on northern Baffin Island, while the "Eskimos don't scold or reprimand their children...the subtle methods of parents in dealing with youngsters are much more effective than the shouting or slapping which some white people use towards naughty children." Theirs was a gentle, patient but relentlessly persistent process of leading children toward reason and reasonable behavior. Desirable behavior was constantly reinforced with love and praise and little bribes. Undesirable behavior was curbed by coaxing, teasing, shaming, or simply by disapproving silence.

The beginning and basis of this infinitely patient and gentle way of rearing children were security and love. Cozy in its mother's amaut, the baby was in constant reassuring contact with her body. There were no fixed feeding times and no frustrations. Whenever it was hungry, it was nursed. It received love and affection not only from its parents, but also from its siblings, in fact, from everyone in camp.

Then comes the age, from one to two, when the child is both very cute and very annoying. Too small to play outside, too big for permanent confinement in the amaut, it creepy-crawls around with surprising speed, gets into everything, grabs everything, explores everything, wants everything and, unless closely watched, will try to swallow nearly everything. It is that period in a white child's life when the most frequent word it hears is "Don't!"

That word, and the harsh tone of command in which it is usually delivered in white society, is virtually absent in traditional Eskimo life. When Archibald Fleming in 1914 at Lake Harbour commented to a woman about the naughtiness of her little boy "she only smiled at me and said: 'He will learn.'" And in Alaska, in 1913, Diamond Jenness watched an Eskimo woman trying to sew while her "two-year-old baby toddled around her, grabbing at her knife and anything else that attracted its attention. Some things she allowed it to keep until it lost interest in them; others she gently took away, but immediately soothed the child with an equivalent." It is a time of patience and of watchfulness, a time of frequent warnings rather than interdicts. "The stove is hot. If you touch it, it will hurt." Sooner or later, of course, the child does touch the stove, gets hurt, cries, receives little sympathy, and henceforth not only leaves the stove alone but is more responsive to its mother's quiet warnings.

Slowly, softly, ever so gently, the child is pushed in the right behavioral direction. If it behaves, if it does well, it is profusely praised. If it bullies, if it screams, its demands no longer elicit an instant positive response. Instead, there may be a seeming indifference to its assertive outburst, a chilly, reproving silence. This change in the emotional atmosphere has a very sobering effect on children. They curb their willfulness. They learn to comply with general attitudes. There still is, there always is, that warm embracing love, of the parents and the others in the camp. But, as the child turns three, the gentle, affectionate badinage, the blandishments, the honeyed words of subtle persuasion, change, nearly imperceptibly, in tone. A child who misbehaves is teased; a tantrum is met with mocking mimickry; derisive laughter shames the child; it is even threatened with bogeymen and separation.

In Greenland in the 1860s, according to the Danish scientist Henry Rink, children were never punished "but threatening them with the vengeance of malevolent spirits was one of the means employed to keep unruly urchins in check." There were the "Kungusu-tarissat," the chilly-slimy mermen, notorious for abducting "petulant and disobedient children." There, remote but more real, were the "erkigdlit," the fearsome Indians, the Eskimos' ancestral enemies and their favorite bogeymen from Alaska to East Greenland. But any other bugaboo would do, including a resident or passing kabloona (white man). At one camp where I lived, I was baffled by the behavior of a little girl. Each time I came into her parents' tent, she shrank from me with obvious apprehension and dislike. The reason for this became clear to me when one day, to my dismay, I heard her mother say "and if you don't behave the white man will take you away."

Such threats, however farfetched and implausible, were nevertheless effective because they carried with them the connotation of parental and societal disapproval, coupled with a strong hint at that ultimate sanction, separation. If the child with its assertiveness and demands impinged upon the individual freedom of the adults, the adults retaliated by threatening the child's sense of security. The Eskimo method of bringing up children, noted Jean Briggs, was "highly consistent." The demands "were always the same: control

of emotionality, generosity, helpfulness, honesty, independence." This "demand for control (i.e. self-control and reasonableness), though clothed in the mildest voice, was...relentless. The lesson takes a remarkably short time to learn, judging from the almost infallible control of the children." In terms of achieving the desired behavioral results with a minimum of overt force, noise and pain, the Eskimo method was extremely efficient. "I have never seen an Eskimo child disobey," wrote the anthropologist E.W. Hawkes in 1914 after a long sojourn on the Labrador coast. "The feeling between children and parents appears to be one of mutual respect and goodwill. The underlying psychology seems to be sound..." And, at the other extreme of the continent, at Point Barrow in the 1880s, scientists of the International Polar Expedition, living in close contact with the Eskimos for more than two years, fell completely in love with the children: "a more obedient and better lot of children cannot be found in all Christendom."

Independence, freedom, individuality, those were, in former days, the basic tenets of Eskimo culture, and children acquired considerable autonomy very early in life. "...there is [among Eskimos] a strongly stated overt value of noninterference in the life of others, even of a child..." the psychologist Arthur E. Hippler has pointed out. The child was not a vassal of its parents but, like its parents, a free and independent being, requiring only occasional guidance due to its inexperience with life and the culturally accepted norms of its society. When Captain G.F. Lyon stopped in 1824 at the Savage Islands off southern Baffin Island to buy artifacts, he was startled to find that, in order to purchase toys, he had to deal with their young owners. The parents merely "advised them in their bargains."

While children had a great deal of independence and were, within the bounds of culturally accepted behavior, free to do whatever they pleased, they were also very much part of the adult world. In the close intimacy of camp life, there were no secrets between adults and children, no divisions based on age. Grown-ups and children alike shared hardships as well as happiness and, of course, the extensive travels of former days. The Netsilingmiut, wrote Rasmussen, "thought nothing of starting on a...journey, which might last for years..." And in 1902, when the British explorer David Hanbury planned to cross the Barrens in midwinter, a trip many of his contemporaries considered just short of suicidal, he was surprised to learn that his Eskimo helpers would travel with their families, including a new-born baby which, he wrote with self-deprecating irony, was coming along "to help explore part of the bleak Northland."

If the children played together much of the time, forming a busy little subtribe of their own, it was by choice, and not due to exclusion from the adult sphere or by parental fiat. Their freedom was well-nigh absolute, their playground infinite in space. "Eskimo children are free to do whatever they like as soon as they can walk," wrote the Oblate priest Raymond de Coccola. Their superb fur clothing protected them from the arctic cold. Recalled Pitseolak, the Cape Dorset artist: "...we never stayed inside much. We had warmer clothes in those days and it used to be fun when it was windy. The fathers would make toy sleds for their sons and daughters...and they would play outside most of the day. Now [the children] are in school all day and they have the habit of staying indoors."

Theirs was a timeless, happy life. On Herschel Island, north of the Yukon, in the spring of 1925 "no matter where one turned, there were children running about, day and night," wrote Captain Henry Larsen, and Diamond Jenness said "the little children were no more bound to a definite bedtime than their parents: they just lay down and slept whenever and wherever they felt inclined." They often "vanished for several hours, and returned in the early

morning...merely to eat and rest before their next excursion. Their parents imposed no restraints on them and exacted no duties." The children at the camp on northern Baffin Island where the writer Doug Wilkinson lived in 1953, were just as free. "There were no regular hours for eating or sleeping. Everyone went to bed when he was tired, ate when he was hungry." The children always played together "and the older ones kept an eye on the younger. The very small children played under the watchful eye of the mother, or an older sister or neighbor...Often the children roamed the land for twenty-four to thirty-six hours at a time without eating or sleeping." The parents worried a bit but said: "The children are happy, and after all, is this not the highest thing to be had from life."

The children, as a rule, played together in quiet harmony. Most of their games were noncompetitive; they played with each other, not against one another. John Murdoch noticed in Alaska in 1881 that the children "...attend quietly to their own affairs and their own amusements." One frequent source of strife in other cultures, possessiveness—"this is MY doll!"—was virtually absent. Children were taught from infancy to share, constantly saw adults share, and lived in a society that attached great value to good behavior and little importance to possession. "Games [among children] never seem to lead to quarrels," wrote the Finnish geographer V. Tanner after spending a long time on the Labrador coast in the 1930s, and F.W. Peacock, superintendent of Moravian missions pointed out "...among Labrador Eskimos there is an absence of competitive games which gratify the self-assertive or mastery impulse...the team idea is lost in the individualism that marks the Eskimo play." And, half a continent away, the children at Jean Briggs' camp also played together with "little competition and less quarreling."

Eskimo children had a wide variety of toys and many games. In 1929 the Danish scientist Therkel Mathiassen and his young assistant,

Frederica de Laguna, who later became a famous anthropologist, dug through a massive midden on the small island of Inugsuk north of Upernavik on the northwest coast of Greenland. As they worked their way through layer after layer, slowly stripping away the accumulated debris of more than eight centuries, it became clear to them that "these Eskimos certainly loved their children, for we found toys everywhere." They unearthed 101 dolls, "...more dolls than specimen of any other type." Most of the toys and games, some made nearly a thousand years ago, were strikingly similar to those used by Eskimo children until recently. They also found that the children's toys "mirrored the culture of their parents so fully that we could have learned the essential character of this culture [Thule] if only the toys had been found. Some of the toys were small implements which the children could have used." Others were beautifully made miniature replicas of the hunting weapons and the domestic implements used by the adults, among them "harpoons, bows and arrows, bird darts, lances, bladder darts, sledges, kayaks, umiaks, knives, snow shovels, adzes, mattocks, cooking pots and lamps, meat trays, spoons, platform mats...Anybody could see that the parents loved their children and delighted to make toys for them." Whenever an Eskimo father had a leisure hour, said Freuchen, he carved toys for his children "a doll for the girls, animal figurines for the boys," or small sleds and hunting weapons. Captain Leopold M'Clintock, searching for traces of the missing Franklin expedition on King William Island in 1859 came upon several abandoned Eskimo houses. In one he found "a child's toy, a miniature wooden sled..." It was made of wood from one of Franklin's ships.

Most of the children's games were imitations of their future adult roles. The boys "hunted," the girls "mothered" their dolls and "kept house." "The boys early receive small harpoons and bows and arrows, and try their skill on small birds and floating pieces of wood. The sling is a favorite amusement in summer, when myriads of waterfowl visit the shores," observed E.W. Hawkes in 1914 in Labrador. "Little girls 'keep house' with [their dolls] in little snow iglus in winter or in old tent circles in summer. I saw...a playhouse [at a summer camp] with its little fireplace and lamp of brightly coloured pebbles and [a] bed of moss..." Thousands of miles to the west, on Victoria Island in 1915, Jenness watched adults and children at play: "While the adults amused themselves at archery beside the camp, the children played their own games on the slope above. They set up fences of turf to enclose fictitious caribou, and dug shallow pits from which to shoot their arrows; or they marked out a line of snow-huts with pebbles, and filled the dance-house with imaginary singers. Thus the occupations of the parents were the pastimes of the children, who learned in play their duties of after years." The children were extremely observant and expert little mimics. They learned, the anthropologist Asen Balikci remarked, "from adults and from older children in the typical Eskimo manner—through observation, collaborative performance, and imitation."

Like children everywhere, they had special rhymes and jingles to accompany some of their games. At Point Barrow in 1913, Jenness recorded one the children chanted when playing hide-and-seek:

"Heads together, heads together,
Stand with your heads together.
She is hiding beyond the brook,
She is hiding beyond the brook.
Let us look for her. Come."

And in 1922 at Igloolik Rasmussen saw two little girls skip in rhythm with this steadily repeated little rhyme, their skipping rope made of seal thong:

"Bring hither your wooden hair ornament,
I will deck myself with it,
To make me look like a real woman."

Games were loved by young and old for, as an

A bright blond Lapp boy in national dress.

A little Lapp girl in Norwegian Lapland.

An Indian girl at Rupert's House.

An Eskimo girl squints in the brilliant light of spring.

Following page:
Eskimo family holding service at home on Sunday.

103

An Indian boy from Rupert's House on the James Bay coast, intent on making a drawing in school.

An Eskimo boy concentrates on his school work.

Following page:
Story telling time in a Repulse
Bay school for Eskimo children
in the far north.

Lapps read the Bible on Sunday.

Eskimo mother and child at an Anglican service.

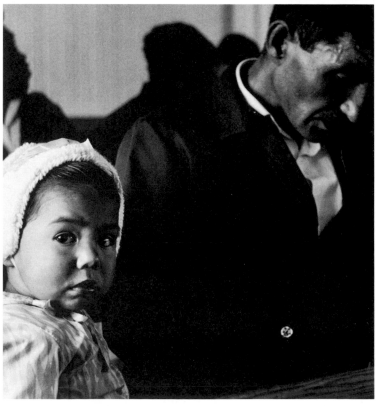

While her elders pray, a pensive Indian girl stands in the doorway of the church.

A little Eskimo girl with her father in a Moravian church on the Labrador coast.

Eskimo children romp outside during recess.

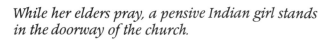

110

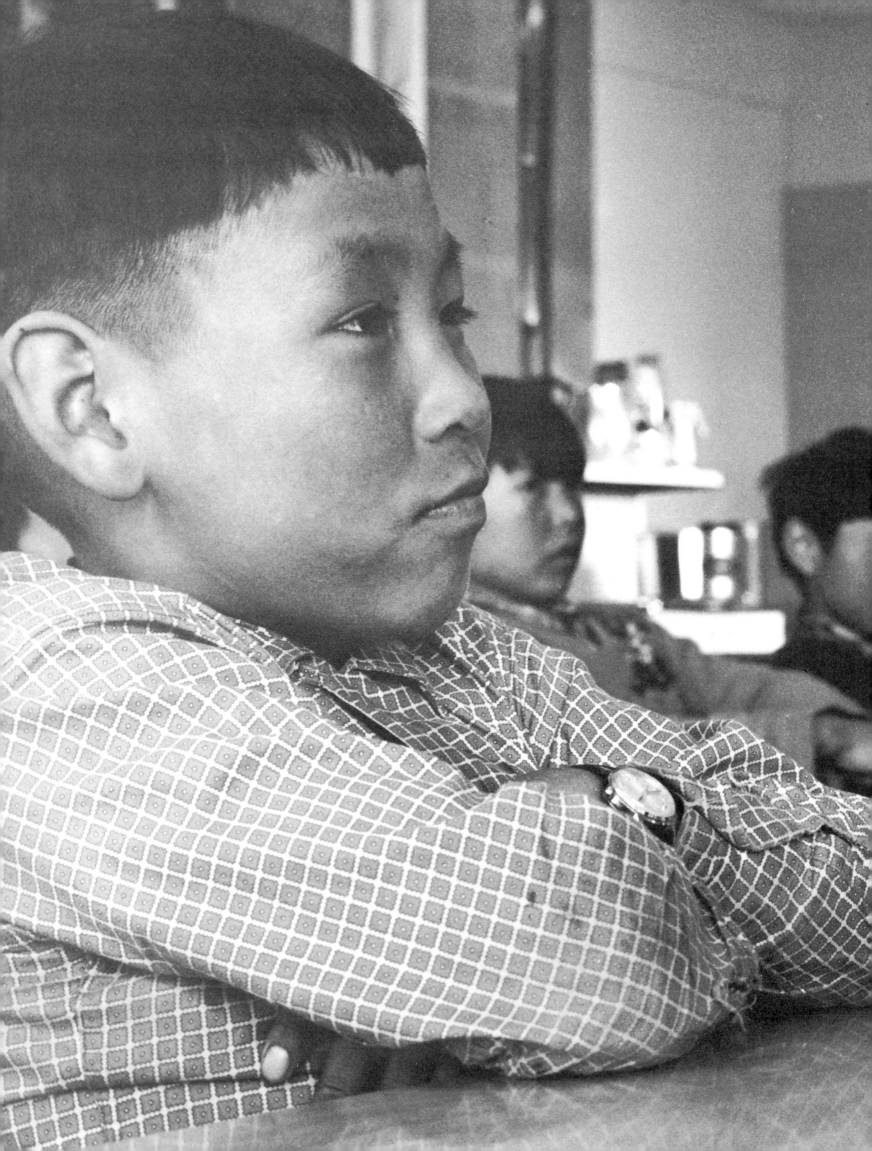

Eskimo proverb says "those who know how to play can easily leap over the adversities of life." Some games, such as "ajaqaq," akin to cup-and-ball or ring-and-pin required great skill. In its simplest form this consisted of a short piece of hollow bone to which a pointed stick was attached by a short sinew string. The player flicked up the bone tube and tried to impale it on the stick. In more intricate versions of this game, a seal or bear carving into which many holes had been drilled, was used instead of the bone tube. Since some holes were easy to hit and others very difficult, a whole scoring system went with these variants of the ajaqaq game.

A favorite game until recently was "nuglutang" which Franz Boas watched in the 1880s on Baffin Island. "A small, rhomboidal of ivory with a hole in the center is hung from the roof and steadied by a heavy stone or piece of ivory hanging from its lower end. The Eskimos stand around it and when the winner of the last game gives a signal everyone tried to hit the hole with a [sharpened] stick. The one who succeeds has won. This game is always played amid great excitement."

They had whirligigs, teetotums and tops, and "mitigligaun," the Eskimo equivalent of a bean-snapper which, John Murdoch somewhat ruefully reported, "is purely an instrument of mischief." It was a ruler-shaped strip of baleen, strong yet flexible, with a slight indentation at one end. "It is held in the left hand, a little pebble is set in the socket, and the tip of the whalebone [baleen] bent back with the right hand. When this end is let go the elasticity of the whalebone drives the pebble at the mark with considerable force." Most of these games are ancient; they were played in the far north since the dawn of man. Among the more than 100 cat's cradle figures Eskimos know how to make, one is called "kalifaiciaq" in the western Arctic and "kilifagssuk" by Greenland's Polar Eskimos. It represents the long-extinct mammoth, whose memory lives on in this string figure which

northern man first made thousands of years before Rome was founded or Babylon was built.

The most intricate toys were made in Alaska and the western Canadian Arctic, animal puppets equipped with baleen springs. John Murdoch admired them at Point Barrow in 1881. A toy fox and raven were moved with sinew strings which activated the baleen springs "so that the fox sprang at the raven and the raven pecked at the fox." Nuligak remembered these puppets vividly from his early youth, when winter was a "time of dancing and rejoicing which began with the departure of the sun and ended with its return." Young and old assembled in the "kradjgierk," the spacious communal house built of driftwood, sod and snow, its ceiling nearly twelve feet high. There, in the yellowish, flickering light of the oil lamps the children watched, intrigued and fascinated, as the animal puppets performed. "...a swan hopped over the door sill. It walked into the middle of the floor, stopped, fluttered its wings...looking here and there, stretching and bending its long neck...[we] could have sworn it was a real swan." Then "a white fox paraded about, going so far as to eat fish scraps from a woman's rubbish box—it really seemed to eat." The older people who made these toys worked only at night, so the children would not see them, since that would have spoiled the marvel and the magic of these performances. "There were a great variety of these puppets: white bears, brown bears, foxes of all colours, weasels, ducks—and to think that all of them moved as though they were alive!" These toys are long forgotten. Diseases brought by whalers spread rapidly from camp to camp. "Before we youngsters could learn from the old, a severe illness carried them away," wrote Nuligak. With them died the ancient knowledge, handed down through untold generations, of how to make these ingenious baleen spring puppets.

In the Footsteps of My Father

Far to the west, above Siberia, the sun sank slowly below the horizon in a final burst of crimson splendor, setting the wispy mare's-tail clouds aglow and silhouetting the massive dark shape of Russia's East Cape. The pack ice hemmed us in. We had pulled our umiak, a 30-foot skin-covered boat, onto a large floe and now we were drifting northward with the pack through Bering Strait toward the Chukchi Sea, prisoners of the ice. The Eskimos seemed unconcerned. These were men from Little Diomede, that small, bleak, craggy island in the midst of Bering Strait, halfway between Alaska and Siberia, perhaps the most-skilled and daring hunters of the north. June is their most important hunting month, the month, they say, "when people do not sleep." It is the month when the vast walrus herds migrate north from the Bering to the Chukchi Sea, all funneling through Bering Strait. Here men from Little Diomede have hunted them each spring, with umiaks similar to ours, for a thousand years and perhaps much longer, for Ignaluk, the tiny village tacked to the slope of their soaring granite island, has been inhabited for at least twenty centuries.

There were 13 people in our boat, eleven hunters and one boy, and I, a tolerated supernumerary. For Tommy, the 11-year-old boy, this was his first hunting season with the men and, like me, he was partly thrilled and partly apprehensive. Most of the crew were his close relatives, uncles and cousins. The captain of our boat, the "umialik," was his father, a stern, decisive man, famous as a hunter, boat builder and carver. Back on Diomede, Tommy had been just another boy, going to school, hunting auklets with his slingshot on the mountain, collecting the seaweed that, dried, was used in soups and stews, and playing with the other children. Now, in the boat, he was a man.

For years, like other boys, he had watched the men leave Diomede in their umiaks, in storm and fog and racing ice, to hunt walruses in Bering Strait, these men whose ruthless courage had earned them the name "the Vikings of the Arctic Sea." Now he was one of them. Tommy and I, as respectively the youngest and the most useless members of the crew were, in a way, a pair, and the men treated us with a nice mixture of solicitude, badinage and camaraderie. They taught us the lore of the pack, the signs that presage storms, the ways of the walrus. They chaffed us for our fears and clumsiness, but watched that we did not get into trouble. Above all, they used praise to bolster our pride. "Tommy's really tough," said one man to another, loud enough so the boy could hear it, or, about me, somewhat more ambiguously "he's not as bad as I expected," and, of course, Tommy and I glowed in their praise and resolutely suppressed all secret yearnings for a warm bed back ashore.

We slept in the umiak on the ice, some curled up in the bottom of the boat, some stretched out on the thwarts. The drum-tight skin cover of the umiak acted as resonator, magnifying the myriad noises of the pack: the creak and groan of grinding floes; the faint lap of water rippling against the ice; the distant roar of walruses, drifting north, like us, upon the floes; the sibilant, urgent whistling wings of oldsquaw ducks, flying in small flocks low over the ice; and the bugling calls of sandhill cranes migrating in chevron formations high in the luminous sky toward their nesting grounds in Siberia.

In the morning the pressure slackened, the ice spread, soot-black leads and pools opened among the floes. We made tea and ate "kauk," walrus skin aged in subterranean caches for a year, then boiled—crunchy, fatty, and immensely energy-rich. The men dispersed along the edge of our large floe and scraped the ice with their harpoon shafts. The grating noise travels far in the water and often attracts curious seals to within shooting range. Tommy and I remained near the umiak; Tommy plinking with his .22 at anything that flew or swam, including, to my distress, the ethereally beautiful ivory gulls which I dearly would have liked to photograph. Suddenly a seal surfaced near our floe. Tommy steadied his rifle on a chunk of ice, took careful aim and shot it through the head. It was his first seal, he had killed it instantly and now it began to sink. We tried to launch the boat. It was too heavy. But the men, always alert, noted our futile efforts, guessed the reason and came racing across the ice to help us. They pushed the umiak into the water and snagged the sinking seal with a weighted hook. Tommy was elated. The men made much of it. Even his father who was often gruff and curt, praised his skill. He was a hunter now and they spoke to him as an equal.

To the northeast of us was water sky, those sombre, brooding clouds that are the sign of open sea. We zigzagged through the leads and lanes among the floes. On a large pan near the edge of the pack, walruses were sleeping. The men paddled stealthily to the floe then, at a whispered word from the umialik, fired together at close range. Five walruses slumped in death, the others lumbered off the floe, bellowing in fear and fury.

The men cut up the massive carcasses with incredible speed and precision. The weather was changing fast. Ragged storm clouds scudded across the sky. Tommy and I, drenched in sweat and smeared with blood, helped to haul the great chunks of meat to our boat, three tons of meat and hide and ivory. Grey fog oozed across the ice and sea and enwrapped us like a clammy shroud. We headed south-southwest. The wind increased, the boat pitched and lurched in the rising waves. They raised the yard-broad waistcloth, furled against the gunwale in calm seas, on paddles and poles around the boat and lashed it securely as a guard against the wind-whipped spray. The day dragged on toward a dark and evil night. We had been at sea already for more than 50 hours in an open boat and now the storm was upon us. One man stood in the bow to watch for the ice floes that surged suddenly out of the murk and spume, drifted past, phantom shapes in the gloom, and vanished again into the grey void that surrounded us.

Tommy and I sat together on the food box toward the stern of the umiak, lolling against each other with the wildly yawing motion of the boat, dozing fitfully, chilled to the very core. I could feel Tommy shiver in uncontrollable spasms, but when I put a protective arm around him and pulled him towards me, he shook me off and muttered an indignant "No!" One does not hug a man! Later, though, toward midnight, when the storm was at its peak, flinging sheets of spray across the waistcloth and icy water soaked us to the skin, one of the men crept towards us from thwart to thwart, like a huge dark crab, took off his great parka, wrapped it tightly around the boy, gave us an encouraging grin, and crawled back to his seat, now only dressed in shirt and pullover.

Toward morning, the storm abated. The fog began to scatter and in the distance we saw the soaring granite walls of Diomede. Three hours later we were home. The men unloaded the boat; a flock of children watched us. One of the men reeved a rope through the lower jaw of Tommy's seal and he marched off, a little man, dead tired but proud, hauling home his seal.

Now the seal was eaten by his family and a few pieces of it were sent to the closest relatives. In former days on Diomede, as elsewhere in the Arctic, a boy's first seal was an event that was exuberantly celebrated.

117

Each person in the village received a small piece of the seal and the boy thus became symbolically the provider of the entire group. He was the hero of the feast that followed and, now a man amongst men, he learned the joy of sharing and to savor its reward, prestige. "The Eskimos held in the highest esteem a generous man who was always ready to give of what he had," noted the anthropologist Nelson Graburn, who lived with the people along Hudson Strait.

Among the Netsilingmiut on King William Island, Rasmussen observed in 1923 "it is a very important event, and one to be celebrated, when a small boy catches his first fish." One little tyke, only six years old, stood unflinchingly in the ice-cold, rushing water. When he speared his first char, his mother cried loudly, joyfully that her son had caught a fish "and the day was celebrated with a great feast." And the first caribou killed by a boy of the Umingmaktormiut of Bathurst Inlet "had to be eaten by everybody in the village." It was a joyous, happy rite, a time to share, and feast, and praise, and children thus learned early, as the Inuk author Minnie Aodla Freeman recalled, that "pleasing others was a pleasure."

They started young. Among the Aleuts, boys of twelve learned to hunt with kayaks in a region which, according to the U.S. Coast Pilot, has "the most unpredictable [weather] in the world. Winds of up to 90 miles an hour are commonplace...howling storms may be expected at any time during the year." At Point Barrow in 1881, the biologist John Murdoch observed that "boys of six or seven begin to shoot small birds and animals and to hunt for birds' eggs, and when they reach the age of twelve or fourteen are usually intrusted with a gun and seal spear and accompany their fathers to the hunt...One boy not over thirteen years old...had his seal nets set like the men and used to visit them regularly, even in the roughest [winter] weather. Lads of fourteen or fifteen are

sometimes regular members of the whaling crews." And Peter Pitseolak of Cape Dorset recalled that when he was a little boy his father gave him the bow and arrow to shoot at an already mortally wounded caribou. "Maybe somebody held my arms to help me. I shot and grazed the caribou. My family told me I was a great hunter."

Just as Tom Sawyer got his friends to plead with him to let them whitewash the fence by making it appear to be a desirable and prestigious occupation rather than a tedious and debasing job, so did Eskimo parents, with a mixture of subtle prodding and ample praise, get their children to do work eagerly and willingly. There was nothing coercive about it. That would have been alien to the Eskimos' ingrained respect for the individual's freedom to do precisely as he pleased. The parents, indeed the whole society and its culture, simply created an emotional climate in which work became something the children very much wanted to do. Once children reached the age when they no longer wished to appear childish, they adopted quite naturally, and seemingly of their own volition, adult values and participated in adult occupations. Compared to the child labor regulations that once prevailed in more advanced societies, theirs was a gentle, pleasant way of inducing children to work with pride and pleasure. England's Factory Act of 1833 abolished forced labor only for children under six, and limited the working day for others to 16 hours.

Eskimo "education" was more osmotic than didactic. "...children were never separated from their parents for any length of time," noted the anthropologist Asen Balikci. "They grew up in close association with the adult world, free to observe and imitate their parents...learning proceeded exclusively through observations and imitation; no formal teaching whatsoever took place." And Graburn among the Eskimos of Hudson Strait observed that nothing was "particularly forced...the child took its own time to learn things."

Children absorbed already with their language some of the priorities of their society. Time was unimportant. For Eskimos, wrote Mrs. Manning, "time is no cut and dried commodity parcelled out into valuable sections...but a leisurely thing that goes on and on at one's convenience..." Consequently, as the linguist Raymond Gagné has pointed out, "words for time are lacking in Eskimo... [because it] does not have the same relevance in traditional Eskimo culture as it does in our culture." But space and spatial relations within their environment were of the utmost importance to people who travelled far in a seemingly featureless land. Hence, Eskimos "are able to specify, with more precision than is found in most languages, where things and places are located...[and] how to reach them." During the frequent, lengthy travels with their parents the children learned about the land. They memorized the shape of distant mountains, the course of a river, the sequence and shape of lakes they passed. And when they camped, they rushed off to explore, roamed far across the land, yet had no problem finding their way back, for they had learned that vital lesson of the north, to visually remember the environment so that a hundred nearly instinctively retained clues will guide one home. Tests carried out in Alaska by the psychologist Judith Kleinfeld showed that Eskimo children were able to absorb and retain "very small visual clues," that they had "a high level of perceptual skills," remarkable "cognitive abilities," and an "unusual ability to recall visual detail." It is the same highly trained, incredibly retentive visual memory which enables an Eskimo to take a complex motor or a watch apart and, often days later, accurately reassemble it. It was this phenomenal knowledge of their land, acquired gradually through constant observation from infancy on, that so

amazed early explorers and later travelers. "The knowledge that the Esquimaux possess of the geography of their country is truly wonderful," wrote Charles Francis Hall, after living with the people of Baffin Island in the 1860s. In 1914, when Bishop Fleming visited the northwest coast of Foxe Basin, "...Silah drew me an excellent map of the coastline... [by] the poor light from a flickering blubber lamp and two candles." The map differed greatly from the government maps Bishop Fleming had along. Silah looked at these maps and declared that whoever had drawn them was "completely ignorant." He was right. It was his own map, hundreds of miles of complex coastline drawn from memory, that proved to be accurate.

"This geographical knowledge is of course accompanied by a most intimate acquaintance with the animals and their habits—a knowledge on which their whole existence depends," wrote Rasmussen. That knowledge, too, they began to absorb from infancy. Each time the men returned from the hunt they would recount all they had seen and experienced and the others listened with rapt attention. These stories, apart from recreating the drama of the hunt, contained, as a rule, extremely detailed descriptions of the land the men had traversed and vivid accounts of the animals they had seen and what these animals had done. The land, the sea, the animals; to a hunting people these were subjects of never-ending fascination and through their vibrant tales of travelling and of hunting, there was a constant transmission of information from the older to the younger generation. When a young Eskimo speaks about his land and its animals one phrase recurs like a leitmotiv: "my father once told us..." The tremendous freedom they enjoyed made children self-reliant at an early age. This was encouraged. Already very young, they learned to dress, to protect themselves properly from the searing cold. Small tykes used the razor-sharp knives that lay in every tent, to cut up meat or whittle sticks. They learned, often painfully, by doing and the adults praised their efforts and indulgently shrugged off the damage they often caused. An Eskimo woman told Freuchen: "Children ruin things without giving it a thought; they have no cares. But every day of their lives they become wiser and wiser." But if they hurt themselves, or fought with each other and cried, they received scant sympathy from the adults. Eskimos believe, said Minnie Aodla Freeman, that "if one is sympathized with, one will grow up with a mixed-up nature, aggressive and demanding attention...So if one of us cried at home, it was a waste of tears." Many of the skills they would require as adults to survive and succeed in their harsh and demanding land, they acquired as youngsters through play. "As young children we amused ourselves by trying to build igloos. Thus I learnt the art," Nuligak recalled. A favorite diversion of the children was catching little fish, polar cod or sculpins, and this helped them to develop both the patience and dexterity they would need later in life in the hunt of larger game. At the camp where Jean Briggs lived there were three little girls and they were forever busy. They helped with fishing and cleaned the fish; they gathered heather for the fire; they roamed far across the tundra; they slithered across the smooth ice of a lake in fall; they "chased lemming and ermine with wild torrents of giggles in and out and around their stony burrows"; they stalked ptarmigan and killed them with stones; they harnessed themselves to small sleds, taking turns being "dogs" and "driver"; they played at caribou stalking and butchering; they made "stuffed dolls out of scraps of cloth and hide"; they sewed clothes for their dolls; they set up a tent and played "house"; and they fried bannock for themselves. The adults rarely interfered in the children's activities. There were none of the "do's and don't's" that constantly prick at children in white society. With increasing skill came pride in their

achievements, a sense of importance and assurance. In 1916, Diamond Jenness with one companion set out on a two-week walk across the tundra to an Eskimo camp. Earlier he had lived with an Eskimo family for a year and now he asked their daughter, Jennie, to come along. "[She] was the merriest of companions, and the most useful...Her laughter was infectious, and no merrier party ever tramped those northern meadows. She was only twelve years of age...with all a child's love of play, [yet] she insisted on performing all the duties that her mother would have undertaken...

She gathered fuel for our campfire...she superintended...the cooking of our evening meal...she dried our marching boots...and patched any holes that the stones might have cut in their soles. She shot an eider duck...Altogether, her education was remarkably adapted to the country in which she lived..."

They went with their parents on long migrations, they ran and romped and climbed, and they became resilient, proud and strong. "Their hardiness is something wonderful," marvelled the anthropologist E.W. Hawkes in 1914 in Labrador. "I have seen them in the early spring...running up and down the beach, and splashing and wading in the icy water, perfectly naked, and evidently having the time of their lives." In 1915, when Jenness migrated with "his" Eskimo family across part of Victoria Island, both adults and children carrying heavy loads, Jennie, the little girl, then 11 years old, stumbled against a stone and bruised "her knee so severely that she limped for two or three days; but when someone asked her if she were hurt she straightened up resentfully and marched ahead without a tear." And at Jean Briggs' camp when the adults departed for the autumn caribou hunt, during which they would walk across the rugged tundra for hundreds of miles, they left the old people and small children in camp. But one little girl of six was permitted to come along, because the previous year she had been left behind and had been sad. "She was a valiant little figure in her red parka as she plodded off over the hummocky tundra, already far behind the others before they were out of sight of the camp."

With such an early training, it was small wonder that the children of the north grew into men and women of extraordinary stamina and strength. The Eskimo hunters with whom David Hanbury lived on the Barrens in 1901 often left "long before daylight, without any breakfast...and they would go without food of any kind for forty or forty-eight hours, and think nothing of it." And in Alaska in 1881 John Murdoch noted in amazement that the Eskimos frequently "made journeys of 50 or 75 miles on foot without stopping to sleep." When the occasion required it, they were capable of sustained and nearly superhuman effort. They were equally good at simply doing nothing. As Rev. Peacock put it: "[Before] the white man...invested the Eskimo with much of his own feverishness," the people knew the "joy of idleness." The Eskimos, noted Jean Briggs, are "not as restless as kaplunas, [and] do not feel the need to fill every moment with an activity." In many ways, theirs was a life of extremes: of famine or abundance; of great travels and violent exertions during hunts and of inactivity and confinement at home during prolonged storms; of infinite space without and extremely limited space within their homes. Under conditions in which white men would soon have gone stir crazy, Eskimos lived in relaxed, comfortable harmony. That, too, they learned as children, to quietly occupy themselves in an extremely cramped environment, if need be for days on end, without fidgeting or fighting. In Alaska Sally Carrighar visited an Eskimo home in which "the parents and ten growing children lived in two little rooms. Blizzards at times kept the children indoors for days, and isn't the picture one of staggering pandemonium? There was none. The boys kept them-

selves busy making snares, or toy boats or airplanes; the girls helped with the household work or played with their dolls or the baby. The children of the Utkuhikhalingmiut with whom Jean Briggs lived "were usually gentle-mannered...they were never chittery in the noisy manner of children in my own world." She was amazed at the capacity of a six-year-old girl "for absorbing herself in scarcely perceptible pursuits for hours on end...demanding no attention from anyone."

They sat on the sleeping platform, quietly relaxed, they sang old songs, they talked, they worked, they played—I once watched an Eskimo mother show her little girl how to make cat's cradle figures and they kept it up, happily amused, for many hours—and they slept. Children and adults were capable of doing with little or no sleep for amazingly long periods of time when hunting or travel demanded it, or when they were having so much fun with something, they just hated to go to bed. But if the weather was bad and there was nothing to do, they loved to sleep, long and guiltlessly, for they believed that ample sleep, from time to time, was good for a person.

Until they were five or six years old, boys and girls, as a rule, played together. Then their interests and their play activities began to diverge toward their future adult roles. Many things they continued to do in common: together they gathered dwarf willow and heather for the campfire; they fetched water, or snow and ice in winter; they picked berries; they caught fish; they roamed the tundra in search of birds' eggs; they collected shellfish at low tide, they helped their parents to cut up meat or fish and spread it out to dry. But increasingly their respective occupations, in play or work, were patterned upon those of the adult world, the model and mirror of their future lives.

Girls mothered dolls, sewed clothes for them and played at keeping house. At a very early age they began to help their mothers for, as

Freuchen said, "it took a long time to teach them the many chores a woman must do." They looked after smaller children. "Girls often play a surrogate-mother role for younger brothers and sisters," noted the anthropologist David Damas. While her mother was away checking traps, a small girl at a camp where Jenness lived, watched her baby brother. She "discharged her responsibility most faithfully; whether she played with the child inside the house on the bed skins, or outside in the snow, she never abandoned it for a single moment." And in Alaska in 1881, John Murdoch observed, "little girls often...carry the infants around on their backs...It is no unusual sight to see a little girl of ten or twelve carrying a well-grown, heavy child in this way." Girls learned to scrape skins, to make sinew thread, they were shown how to cut skins into the traditional patterns required for parkas and pants, they cooked, they gathered greens. Much of their work they acted out initially as play, but with increasing age and proficiency, they became their mothers' helpers, performing a wide range of tasks with nonchalant skill. At one camp where I lived, I was given my own seal oil lamp, for warmth and light. No matter what I did with it, it either smouldered darkly, just on the verge of death, or flared up, spewing soot. Then a little girl of ten came to my aid. She took the small, hammer-shaped wick trimmer, tamped and adjusted the moss wick, and within a minute the lamp burned with a beautifully even flame.

While girls thus learned at an early age to emulate their mothers, boys learned to be hunters, with their fathers as their models and their mentors. The father, as a rule, was viewed with considerable respect and often admiration. He was never a "chum" to his children. An Eskimo woman in Alaska explained to Sally Carrighar, "an Eskimo father never tries to act young. He doesn't pretend he is another boy with his son...A child doesn't know what to think if his father acts like a boy one day, and the next day he demands respect."

At first, hunting was a game. Their fathers made them bows and arrows and boys stalked ground squirrels and small birds, usually with endless patience rewarded by rare successes. Among the Polar Eskimos they played "hunting polar bear," one boy being the bear, others the hunters and dogs who pursued the bear, held it at bay and rushed in for the "kill." Or they went "utoq" hunting: one boy was the seal that slept upon the ice, while the others stalked it with patience and finesse. They harnessed young huskies to small sleds; the pups learned to pull and the boys to drive and control them. In early summer, quick as fleas, they hopped from floe to floe near shore, learning to judge the strength of ice, acquiring skills and knowledge that some day might be vital.

At the age from ten to twelve, they began to accompany their fathers. They helped to ice the runners, to load and lash the sled; they watched the sled dogs while the father stalked a seal; the father built the igloo, they filled the chinks with snow. As their skills increased, they were given increasingly complex tasks, praised for success and mildly chaffed for failure. They learned by constant observation, by doing, and, perhaps most indelibly, by making mistakes. At Arctic Bay on Baffin Island in the early 1960s, the teacher Margery Hinds recalled, two boys, one 11 the other 16, went by dog team to check their father's trap line one week when he was ill. While the older boy inspected the traps, the younger watched the dogs. But, lulled by their apparent docility, he did not pay enough attention and suddenly they bolted. The boys walked home at 30 below, without any food, non-stop for a day and a night. And, while all were glad to have them back, they did not escape those sarcastic comments that are the lot of everyone whose dogs have taken off, doubly humiliating for boys entrusted with their father's team.

122

A Lapp boy ties on his boots.

Opposite:
*A Polar Eskimo boy shoots an
arrow into the air with a bow
his father made for him.*

Following page:
*Children on Little Diomede
Island try to catch gulls.
In the background is Siberia.*

Thus, early, usually eagerly, sometimes painfully, the children acquired the skills and knowledge of their parents. Childhood merged into adolescence and into adulthood. There were no rites of passage, no sharp divisions between the ages. Just as time flowed on, unmeasured and uncounted, so did their lives, through all the generations, flow on, the past merging with the present and stretching toward the future in patterns that were nearly immutable. The wisdom and the ways of the adults became, with little change, those of their children, just as their myths and legends were passed from generation to generation with utmost fidelity.

Winters in the far north are gloomy and depressing. Days and nights are dark, the cold intense, storms frequent, hunting and travel curtailed. To counteract the many stresses of these oppressive months, the Eskimos made winter their most sociable and festive season, a time, as Nuligak recalled, "of dancing and rejoicing," a time to sing, a time to tell again the tales of long ago. Pitseolak, the Cape Dorset artist, remembered that when she was young, the people in winter "danced Eskimo dances that went on for a long time—there were no drunks at the dances then." Or they sat quietly at home, while the mother or grandmother told stories that were part ancient cultural lore, part entertainment and could serve at times as lullaby. A Netsilik woman told Rasmussen: "Children are full of life, they never want to sleep. Only a song or monotonous words can make them quieten down so that at last they fall asleep. That is why mothers and grandmothers always put little children to sleep with tales. It is from them we all have our knowledge, for children never forget."

Stories were also told in a more formal setting, in the great "kargi," the communal house or igloo, some large enough to hold sixty to a hundred people. The audience, clad in furs, sat on the ground, oil lamps set in niches cast their flickering, yellowish light over all. The children cuddled close to their parents and listened in fascination to the ancient tales, which never varied an iota. On Baffin Island in the 1880s, Franz Boas attended these evenings filled with tales. "Old traditions are always related in a highly ceremonious manner. The narrator...tells the story slowly and solemnly...The form is always the same, and should the narrator happen to say one word otherwise than is customary he will be corrected by the listeners." It was the same in Greenland where, in the 1860s, Henry Rink observed, "the art requires the ancient tales to be related as nearly as possible in the words of the original version...even the smallest deviation from the original will be taken notice of and corrected" by the audience, familiar, as a rule, from infancy with these beloved tales.

Most of these stories were extremely old and many were known over an area of thousands of miles, from Siberia to East Greenland. Of 52 tales Rasmussen recorded among the Padlermiut of Canada's Barrens, no fewer than 30 were identical to stories he knew from Greenland. At Bathurst Inlet he was told the tale of the adventurous louse. This louse, tired of sitting home, goes off to explore the world, only to be crushed by colliding cliffs (i.e. human finger nails). Rasmussen knew the story from the Thule district of Greenland. Many thousand miles separated the people of Thule and Bathurst Inlet and "for at least a thousand years there had been no communication between them; yet...[by both, identical versions of] this little myth of the louse that never came home had been preserved." While nearly everyone knew a host of tales, some people were famed as storytellers. In some regions of Greenland, said Rasmussen, it was nearly a profession, or at least a way to get free meals for people "who live during winter by telling stories to shorten the long nights..." And when Jenness was in Alaska in 1913, "every large settlement...possessed one or more raconteurs." They told legends and fables and myths, and related, word-perfect, epics so long and intricate "they required three and even four evenings for the telling." Some stories were pure entertainment. When Rasmussen asked Netsit, the master storyteller of the Umingmaktormiut, for the moral of the tale about the fox who teaches the wolf to fish, Netsit replied with a touch of asperity: "It is not always that we want a point in our stories, if only they are amusing. It is only the white men that want a reason and an explanation of everything." This tale, like some other Eskimo stories, has a near-universal theme. The fox has found a salmon and eats it happily. The wolf comes along and eyes him with envy. "How did you catch the fish?" he asks. "Nothing to it," says the fox. "Come, I'll show you." He leads the wolf to a crack in the ice. "Dip in your tail, and when a salmon bites, just yank it out." The wolf, who in all these stories is greedy and gullible, waits long and patiently. It is intensely cold, the water freezes, his tail is stuck and to get free, he pulls so hard, the tail tears off. (In a Lapp version of this story, the bear, who once had a long and bushy tail, gets tricked by the wily fox into using it for fishing, loses it, and ever since bears have tiny tails.)

Many stories, though, were fables with a moral, such as the one about the greedy owl. The owl flies across the tundra and spots two fat hares sitting side by side. It grabs one with each sharply-taloned foot, the hares dash off in different directions, the greedy owl is torn in twain and dies.

Instead of "once upon a time...," these stories, Freuchen said, always began with the traditional words: "In the old days, when people were different from now..." Many of the stories were charming creation legends.

Long, long ago, the raven and the loon decided to tattoo each other. The raven started and did, at first, an exquisite job. But finally his patience gave out and he dumped a pile of ash upon the loon's back, and it still is grey and speckled. The loon, incensed, grabbed a pot of soot and threw it at the raven, and ravens have been soot-black ever since.

A boy lived alone with his grandmother. Once, in his kayak, he was caught by an off-shore storm. For three days and three nights he paddled frantically, turning this way and that. Blood burst from his face and splashed his clothes, and gradually he became transformed into the busily-paddling, rufous-streaked phalarope. His grandmother, who, crying and calling, ran along the shore until her sealskin boots were worn and splayed, was turned into the web-footed loon, whose melancholy cry still quavers across the waters.

A girl and her grandmother lived together in a snow house. One evening, the little girl refused to sleep and kept asking, endlessly, for just one more story. Finally, in exasperation, the old woman shouted that a horde of squirmy, naked lemmings was rushing into the house. Terrified, the little girl flitted out through the entrance passage and turned into the nervously fluttering snow bunting. The grandmother, full of regrets, sobbed and cried until her eyes were red, and she became the carmine-wattled ptarmigan that still sadly bobs and clucks its way across the tundra. Thus passed the long winter evenings, with songs and dances and the telling of those ancient tales that had been transmitted, faithfully, through untold generations. The children listened to them, enthralled, and, some day, would tell them to their children. Now this age-old cycle has been broken. No longer are the children raised in the image of their parents. The legends fade, the fables are forgotten, old traditions die, ancient verities are questioned. The children of the north, descendants of ancient, nearly changeless cultures, are now buffeted by the winds of change.

There Is No Turning Back

The lecture in Toronto was over. I sat down, relieved and slightly sweaty. Someone, appointed to this task, thanked me for my talk. Then came the cocktail party. A huge room filled with milling people. Introductions. Names barely heard and instantly forgotten. A few polite remarks. A couple of vapid questions. A few vague answers. More introductions. More questions. Small talk. The clink of glasses. A haze of cigaret smoke. A blur of faces. The buzz of conversation, social and superficial. And suddenly a soft voice, quite close to me, asked: "Do you remember me?"

He was an Eskimo, a slim young man, conservatively elegant in a pearl-grey three-piece suit and he did not remind me of anyone I knew. He smiled. "I am Joannassie," he said. It was not surprising that I failed to recognize him; the last time I had seen him was many years ago. He was a boy then, dressed in caribou parka, fur mitts and sealskin boots. I had lived for some months at his father's camp on an island nearly a hundred miles from the nearest settlement.

I had been happy at the camp. Joannassie's mother was a warm, generous woman. Her joys in life were her family and food, and from the moment I arrived she had simply added me, like some stray waif, to her family, fussed over me and did her best to fatten me. At every meal, no matter how much I ate, she always urged: "Eat more!" Joannassie's father was broad-shouldered and stocky, immensely strong and enduring. He was quiet and appeared rather stern, and both Joannassie and I stood in considerable awe of him. He was a proud and independent man, and a superb hunter. He had taken us along on many of his trips and we had learned much from him, for he possessed a vast knowledge of this region and its animals.

Joannassie and I drifted toward a quieter corner of the crowded room and reminisced. In this setting our memories of ice and dog teams, of stalking seals and lugging caribou carcasses seemed incongruous and infinitely remote, as of another age, another world. A white-gloved waiter came by with a tray of canapés. "How about some liver?" Joannassie said in Eskimo and we laughed, thinking how horrified these people would be could they have seen us back then, kneeling in the snow around a seal his father had just killed and slit open, eating, in traditional fashion, the warm, blood-dripping liver, together with snippets of blubber.

"I'm sorry about your father," I said awkwardly. "He was a fine man."

Joannassie nodded, his face sombre. "Yes. You heard about it?"

I had not been back to that part of the Arctic, but the grapevine of the north had brought me news of his father's death. In the 1960s the government didn't look kindly upon camps. They were hard to administer and offended the orderly bureaucratic mind. So most camps were closed and the people brought into settlements where adequate housing, schools and good medical services were provided. But with the large population in the settlement, the game resources in the region surrounding it were inadequate to provide the people with food. Joannassie's father could no longer live by hunting. He did odd jobs. He received welfare. Always a quiet man, he became increasingly withdrawn and taciturn. And then he began to drink. One winter night he staggered home from a drinking bout at another house. He stumbled, lay in a stupor and fell asleep. They found him the next day, just a hundred yards from his home, frozen to death.

"What are you doing in Toronto?" I asked.

"Studying," Joannassie said. "I'm going to be a teacher."

"Up north?"

He raised his eyebrows in Eskimo assent.

"I wouldn't want to live in the south."

"But look at you," I teased him. "You are more a Kabloona than an Inuk."

He smiled a trifle bitterly. "Just fifty-fifty. In between."

We spoke of other people I had known. Most had adjusted somehow to settlement life. Some had jobs. Some existed permanently on welfare. A few had left and had gone back to live on the land. Joannassie spoke of them with a certain wistfulness.

"Would you like to go back to the land?" I asked.

"Yes," he said. "The land always pulls us. But you know how it is. I will be a teacher. I can never go back."

Unconsciously, he was echoing the words the brilliant Greenland-born ethnologist Knud Rasmussen had written more than half a century ago, at a time when the land of the Eskimos was still remote and inaccessible and a few groups of Eskimos had only just been "discovered": "When the hand of civilization touches a primitive people anywhere, there is no turning back."

There is no turning back. Their ancient culture has been eroded, their way of life abruptly changed, their very land is threatened. The age-old continuity of their lives in familiar, never-changing patterns has been broken. Theirs is the trauma of transition, the desperate search for a new identity and a new vision. And this vision is totally different from the one held by that other culture, the white man's culture, which increasingly dominates the north.

In November 1978, the Environmental Assessment Review Process panel held hearings in Pond Inlet on northern Baffin Island on the dangers and the desirability of drilling for oil in the bird and sea mammal rich Lancaster Sound. The panel was told by a representative of an air service company, "National interest demands the execution without delay of an exploratory drilling program in Lancaster Sound." He assured the panel that in case of a disaster, his "company would meet any demand on its available resources to assist in bringing a blowout under control."

The Eskimo view was presented by Titus Allooloo, the mayor of Pond Inlet: "Whiteman had said that the North should be developed in such a way that the Inuit will retain their culture. Unfortunately, whiteman's idea of our culture is that we should keep our language so long as we also learn English; keep on carving so that they can own a genuine Eskimo carving; and retain drum dancing to amuse the tourists...if whiteman is really genuinely concerned about our northern culture then he should tread more lightly upon our land. We need the freedom to wander to hunt for food, we need the pleasure of seeing and hearing the thousands of birds that grace our land... yet whiteman will risk the lives of those birds to see what is at the bottom of Lancaster Sound before their knowledge is great enough to drill with absolute safety. It makes me sad this impatience of the whiteman. Because of his impatience there is pollution all over the world."

The pre-European Eskimo, according to anthropologist Diamond Jenness, who had lived for many months with Eskimos who had just been "discovered," was "to a degree that we today can hardly comprehend...free and independent, master of his own fate...healthy... cheerful and relatively contented—far more contented, I believe, than their present-day descendants, or their white fellow countrymen whose restless civilization, with its mélange of virtues and vices they are slowly learning to assimilate."

This is, perhaps, too rosy a view of early Eskimo life. It was hard, precarious, and in some regions haunted by recurring famines. But it did have that saving grace of contentment given to people secure within their society and in harmony with their natural environment. The native people then, said the scientist Dr. Ian McTaggart Cowan, "were a dynamic element in the balanced ecosystem." That balance was broken when southern man came to the north, the explorers first and in their wake the whalers, then traders and missionaries, followed by the vast army of administrators intent upon transforming the north according to their vision, and finally a new wave of explorers, searching this time not for some fabled Strait of Anian that would lead them to Cathay, but for oil and iron and uranium.

The explorers' contact with the natives of the north was prolonged but sporadic and generally superficial. The whalers took from the north much of the wildlife that formed the basis of the Eskimos' existence and they brought to the north a host of diseases to which the natives had little or no immunity. With the whales gone, the whalers went, leaving a land and a sea despoiled of much of its former animal wealth, and a people decimated, many of the survivors wracked by disease, and accustomed to, and dependent upon southern goods. Into the vacuum created by the whalers' departure stepped the fur traders and to pay for the southern goods they had come to regard as essential, the Eskimos became trappers. Where once they had been poor but independent, they were now dependent and still poor, their ancient autarky destroyed beyond redemption.

While these changes were drastic and profound, some of the basic ancestral patterns remained unaltered: the close, nearly mystic relationship with their land, the strong family ties, the traditional way of raising children, the seamless flow of generations. They still lived upon the land and by the land, in more than 700 camps, specks of humanity scattered over the vastness of the north.

It lasted until the 1950s. Then, in less than two decades, a social upheaval of immense proportions took place that tore the ancient fabric of their lives and left its traditions in tatters. In the chill climate of the Cold War, a great number of DEW (Distant Early Warning) Line radar stations were built in the far north. Many Eskimos were employed in their construction and afterward quite a few settled in tents and shacks near these stations, living on odd jobs and handouts. Belatedly, the government realized that it had a problem on its hands.

In resolving this northern problem, the southern government bureaucracy, full of good intentions but essentially paternalistic, unfortunately adopted a "we-must-think-for-them-and-do-what-is-best-for-them" philosophy. The people most directly concerned, the natives of the north, were rarely consulted.

The first step was to concentrate the dispersed population. Settlements were built, most camps were closed and the people moved to the new villages and nascent towns. It was, according to George Swinton, Canada's foremost authority on Eskimo art, "a period of complete cultural and technological change: from dog team to motor toboggan...from disposable architecture [snow house and tent] in over seven hundred camps to permanent housing in some forty-odd urbanized [slum] settlements; from a barter and subsistence economy, in which every family lived off the land, to a mixed welfare and money economy, in which families sell their services or the products of the land in order to obtain money with which to sustain themselves. Failing this —and in some areas as much as eighty per cent of the population are unable to support themselves—money is supplied by the Kablunait [white men] who have come to administer the land."

Since the natives' ways and values were incomprehensible to the white administrators of the north and appeared to them ill suited for the new north as they envisioned it, they sought to create a new society according to their values and their vision. The final goal was assimilation. It was the duty of the whites, said the anthropologists John and Irma Honigmann in a recent work, to act as tutors to the native, to "encourage him to respond in certain definite ways, advise and teach him, withdraw support if he deviates from what they deem appropriate, and reward him if he attains the goal as they see it. In this important type of learning, the Eskimo assumes new roles while the Euro-Canadians observe, correct, reward and punish."

Thus, inevitably, "the world of the native people was altered," wrote Mr. Justice Thomas R. Berger in his report on the Mackenzie Valley pipeline, "whereas the world of the white man—his religion, his economy, his own idea of who he was—remained the same. We sought to make native people like ourselves, and native society like our own; we pursued a policy of cultural replacement. Perhaps nothing offers a better illustration of this policy than the schools we established in the North..."

In 1950, only 120 Eskimo children in all of Canada attended school. Then, big boarding schools were constructed in a few main settlements where children from the small villages and the remaining camps were gathered. Their education was patterned on the curriculums of rural-urban southern Ontario and southern Alberta, and Eskimo children began by learning about "Dick and Jane on the farm." In some schools, they were punished if they spoke their own language. Most of them did not see their parents for nine months of the year.

"Well-meaning professional educationalists working for the government had a field day," observed Northwest Territories Council member Duncan Pryde, "but they never got around to assessing the damage such a system was causing in completely disorienting Eskimo youth from all its cultural background." An Eskimo woman at Arctic Bay on northern Baffin Island told the teacher Margery Hinds: "Those schools change the children so much, that when they come home

again, they are like strangers in the midst of their own families." The ancient cultural continuum had been abruptly severed. Now a chasm separated the generations. This educational policy of the 1950s and 1960s produced, according to Bryan Pearson, mayor of Frobisher Bay on Baffin Island, "a generation of discontented Eskimos, a generation that forever lost its identity, not just as natives but as people."

It was a clash of totally disparate cultures and for the children who were abruptly yanked out of one, their own, to be immersed into another, alien one, it was a wrenching, traumatic experience. They came from a timeless society. Now, like whites, they were slaves of time. They spoke only Eskimo, their teachers spoke only English. They knew only their own arctic world and their own society. Now, suddenly, they were taught about a world far beyond their ken. Among the "educational material" Margery Hinds received for the "newly-opened school for Eskimos" at Arctic Bay, a small community on northern Baffin Island, were these titles "'The conditions of the soil in the state of Texas', 'So you want to be a banker', [and] 'Holidays in Oregon' including an excellent road map for motorists." In most schools the children, shy, apprehensive and bewildered, had hardly gotten used to one teacher when he was replaced by another. Teacher turnover was so rapid, reported the sociologists Charles S. Brant and Charles W. Hobart, that any teacher "who has more than two years of Arctic teaching experience is considered a veteran." And in Alaskan schools teachers came and went with such frequency, the Commissioner of Education complained that teaching there had become "a procession rather than a profession."

It was not easy for the teachers, either. Their pupils, as a rule, were obedient but very quiet and reserved. In keeping with their early training they were observant but not responsive, and even when they did respond they were often misunderstood. At first the children replied to questions requiring "yes" or "no" as an answer with the facial movements of their culture: a slight lifting of the eyebrows signifying "yes," a slight wrinkling of the nose meaning "no." The teachers, unfamiliar with these subtle signs failed to recognize them and became exasperated with their mute pupils, who, in fact, were saying "yes" or "no" in the sign language of their culture. In Eskimo, unlike in English, a negative question is answered in the positive: "You don't have a brother?" "Yes," meaning "Yes, I do not have a brother." This led to endless misunderstandings and to the conviction among some teachers that the children were lying to them. A few lost patience and shouted at the students, which frightened the children and upset their parents, for in traditional Eskimo culture the overt display of anger was rare and feared. "In one remote community," Brant and Hobart found, the Eskimos "were plainly still shocked, two years after the original events, at the fact that a teacher had frequently shouted or screamed at the children." The children came from one culture that frowned on aggressive, assertive and competitive behavior into another that felt that a certain amount of aggressiveness and assertiveness were essential to get ahead in a competitive world. They were constantly taught and exposed to southern values and this, as Brant and Hobart have pointed out, inevitably led them to conclude "that there is nothing in native lore and tradition which is worth learning. Thus this curriculum tends to be destructive of respect for Eskimo values..." As a result of being raised in residential schools, a young Eskimo, Rosemary Kirby, told the Berger inquiry "we grew up to feel ashamed of being Eskimo."

This educational system, whose basic aim was to wean Eskimo children away from their own culture and transform them into useful members of the new society envisioned by the whites, produced, all too often, quite different results. The "best-mannered children in the world," as the biologist Sally Carrighar had called them, ceased to be so under white tutelage and adopted many of the least desirable traits of the new culture. After a visit to Frobisher Bay, the largest settlement on Baffin Island, Attua, the grand old lady of Arctic Bay, confided to Margery Hinds: "I've never known Eskimo children as naughty...They call their parents by bad names, and they won't obey their parents. I spoke to some of the mothers about it and they said there's nothing they can do, their children are merely copying the white children's ways."

Brant and Hobart, studying the effects of the educational system on the natives of the western Arctic, reported that the young Eskimo returning home from a nine months stay in a residential school is "an unhappy, dissatisfied, unadjusted child—almost always described by the word 'cranky' by informants who could speak any English. In contrast to the obedience, respectfulness and helpfulness of Eskimo children in 'unspoiled' communities, such children were disobedient, complaining, disrespectful and reluctant to undertake chores spontaneously or at the indirect hinting of parents in the way which is traditional among Eskimos. They were unable to amuse themselves in a self-contained manner or be contented. Especially marked was the children's loss of respect for parents...

"Other consequences [of education in white schools] mentioned by Eskimo parents [to Brant and Hobart] are lying, stealing, and sneaky behavior, all of them offenses against traditional Eskimo morality and virtually unheard of in the more remote settlements." And in 1960 Margery Hinds noted, "there are already juvenile delinquents among Eskimos nowadays, something unheard of in the days before they attended school."

Adrift between two worlds, unhappy and insecure in both, many of the white-educated young, Brant and Hobart noted, became "drifters who are unable to adapt to the loneliness or the employment conditions of the town, but who despise traditional employments, and live parasitically off the sharing patterns of the community." Many northern natives, the psychologist Pat Kehoe told the Berger inquiry, suffer a psychiatric disorder known as "reactive depression...This disorder is recognized by a set of symptoms including passivity, lack of interest, lack of motivation and ambition, and a feeling of helplessness...this disorder is [now] virtually endemic among the northern native people..." A bitter old Indian woman told the same inquiry that "the white man...has spoiled everything for the native people, even our own children."

In 1973, a survey was made by the CBC in Frobisher Bay and Fort Chimo, two of the largest arctic towns. By this time "little remained of the traditional life style of the Eskimo people in Frobisher Bay...The population had become generally sedentary and were mostly dependent on social assistance." In answer to the question "Most desirable jobs for sons," 16 per cent did not answer, and 48 per cent said they had "no idea." In answer to the question "Most desirable jobs for daughters" 13 per cent did not answer and 49 per cent had "no idea." Fifty-three per cent listed "Alcoholism" as the "leading problem in the community." The children were sent to school in order that they might fit into the new north and to obtain equal and gainful employment in its rapid technological development. But when they graduated, there were few jobs for them. Nor did they have the skills, formerly learned from their elders, and the great practical experience required to become successful hunters. "They exist," said Northwest Territories Council member Duncan Pryde, "in a vacuum between the two ways of life...It is a strange paradox that the formal school education of the Eskimo is directly responsible for the massive unemployment of the native people in the Arctic..." In 1971, in the village of Baker Lake, west of Hudson Bay, there were 122 unemployed teenagers out of a total population of 765.

The children, said Dr. Otto Schaefer, director of the Northern Medical Research Unit, "...were deprived of the ideal image of their parents [and] do not respect them. Having lost any functional role in the Eskimo world without being able to realize the dreams produced from schools and movies, [they] feel useless, and become confused, frustrated and rebellious." With the disintegration of their society and its basic unit, the once close-knit family, the "individual is left insecure, lonely, directionless and meaningless."

The young of the north today are suspended between two worlds, one dear but dying, the other alien yet alluring. They are a people in search of a new identity, a synthesis between the old and new that once again will give their lives meaning and direction and free them from the cultural limbo in which most of them now live.

In 1972, while attending a conference in Pangnirtung on Baffin Island, William Tagoona, a young "city" Eskimo, met some camp Inuit who had come "to town" to do some shopping. Later he wrote about this meeting in the magazine *Inuttituut:* "I was surprised to see how unspoiled and happy they were. I did not feel much of an Inuit beside these happy people and thought to myself 'so these are the real Inuit!' I felt I was an Inuit of today and did not have much in common with the old. My language is still there but what part of me is real Inuit?"

*"I will take care not to go toward the dark.
I will go toward the day."*

*(Ancient magic song of the
Inuit recorded in 1922 by
Knud Rasmussen).*

A little Eskimo girl with her pet pup.   *Three Eskimo girls with their pet pups.*

Preceding page:
Travel in spring along smooth
ice between sea and land in
northwest Greenland; the eldest
boy wields the whip, the other
children walk behind the sled
with their father.

In his imagination, a little boy drives a dogteam like his father.

An Eskimo boy romps with a friendly husky.

Following page:
Eskimo camp at Bathurst Inlet
in fall under a full moon.

Bibliography

Anderson, Sally. "Norway's Reindeer Lapps." National Geographic Magazine, Vol. 152, No. 3 Washington, 1977.

Back, George. "Narrative Of The Arctic Land Expedition To The Mouth Of The Great Fish River And Along The Shores Of The Arctic Ocean In The Years 1833, 1834 And 1835." John Murray. London, 1836. Reprinted by M.G. Hurtig Ltd., Edmonton, 1970.

Baird, Patrick D. "The Polar World." Longmans, Green and Co. Ltd. London, 1964.

Balikci, Asen. "The Netsilik Eskimo." The Natural History Press. Garden City, New York, 1970.

Berger, Thomas R. "Northern Frontier, Northern Homeland." James Lorimer & Co., Publishers. Toronto, 1977.

Boas, Franz. "The Central Eskimo." Published in the 'Sixth Annual Report Of The Bureau Of Ethnology, Smithsonian Institution.' Washington 1888; reprinted by the University of Nebraska Press. Lincoln, 1964.

Bosi, Roberto. "The Lapps." Thames and Hudson. London, 1960.

Brant, Charles A. and Hobart, Charles W. "The Education System In The Western Arctic." In "Eskimo Of The Canadian Arctic," Victor F. Valentine and Frank G. Vallee, editors. McClelland and Stewart Limited. Toronto, 1971.

Briggs, Jean L. "Never In Anger. (Portrait Of An Eskimo Family)." Harvard University Press. Cambridge, Mass., 1970.

Bruemmer, Fred. "Seasons Of The Eskimo." McClelland and Stewart Limited. Toronto, 1971.

Bruemmer, Fred. "The Arctic." Optimum Publishing Co. Ltd. Montreal, 1974.

Burnford, Sheila. "One Woman's Arctic." McClelland and Stewart Limited. Toronto, 1973.

Carpenter, Edmund, et al. "Anerca." J.M. Dent & Sons (Canada) Ltd. Toronto, 1959.

Carpenter, Edmund, et al. "Eskimo." University of Toronto Press. Toronto, 1959.

Carpenter, Edmund and Heyman, Ken. "They Became What They Beheld." Ballantine Books, Inc., New York, 1970.

Carrighar, Sally. "Best-Mannered Children In The World." Saturday Evening Post, Vol. 227, No. 23, December 4, 1954.

Damas, David. "Igluligmiut Kinship Terminology And Behaviour: Consanguines." In "Eskimo Of The Canadian Arctic." Victor F. Valentine and Frank G. Vallee, editors. McClelland and Stewart Limited. Toronto, 1971.

de Coccola, Raymond and King, Paul. "Ayorama." Oxford University Press. Toronto, 1955.

de Laguna, Frederica. "Voyage To Greenland." W.W. Norton & Co. New York, 1977.

Eber, Dorothy, editor. "Pitseolak: Pictures Out Of My Life." Oxford University Press. Toronto, 1971.

Fejes, Claire. "People Of The Noatak." Alfred A. Knopf. New York, 1966.

Fleming, Archibald L. "Archibald The Arctic." Saunders of Toronto Ltd. Toronto, 1965.

Freeman, Minnie Aodla. "Life Among The Qallunaat." Hurtig Publishers. Edmonton, 1978.

Freuchen, Peter. "Arctic Adventure." Farrar & Rinehart Inc. New York, 1935.

Freuchen, Peter. "Ice Floes And Flaming Water." Julian Messner, Inc. New York, 1954.

Freuchen, Peter. "Book Of The Eskimos." Fawcett Publications, Inc. New York, 1965.

Gagné, Raymond C. "Spatial Concepts In The Eskimo Language." In "Eskimo Of The Canadian Arctic," Victor F. Valentine and Frank G. Vallee, editors. McClelland and Stewart Limited. Toronto, 1971.

Graburn, Nelson H. "Eskimos Without Igloos." Little, Brown and Company. Boston, 1969.

Hall, Charles Francis. "Life With The Esquimaux." Samson Low, Son, & Marston. London 1864. Reprinted by Charles E. Tuttle Co.: Publishers. Rutland, 1970.

Hanbury, David T. "Sport And Travel In The Northland Of Canada." Edward Arnold. London, 1904.

Hawkes, E.W. "The Labrador Eskimo." Canadian Department of Mines, Geological Survey, Memoir 91. Ottawa, 1916.

Hinds, Margery. "High Arctic Venture." The Ryerson Press. Toronto, 1968.

Hippler, Arthur E. "Some Observations On Witchcraft: The Case Of The Aivilik Eskimos." In Arctic, Journal Of The Arctic Institute Of North America. Vol. 26, No. 3. Montreal, September, 1973.

Honigmann, John. J. and Irma. "People Under Tutelage." In "Eskimo Of The Canadian Arctic," Victor F. Valentine and Frank G. Vallee, editors. McClelland and Stewart Limited. Toronto, 1971.

Jenness, Diamond. "Dawn In Arctic Alaska." University of Minnesota Press. Minneapolis, 1957.

Jenness, Diamond. "The People Of The Twilight." The Macmillan Co., 1928. Reprinted by The University of Chicago Press. Chicago, 1959.

Jenness, Diamond. "Eskimo Administration: I. Alaska." Arctic Institute of North America, Technical Paper No. 10. Montreal, 1962.

Jenness, Diamond. "Eskimo Administration: II. Canada." Arctic Institute of North America, Technical Paper No. 14. Montreal, 1964.

Jenness, Diamond. "The Economic Situation Of The Eskimo." In "Eskimo Of The Canadian Arctic," Victor F. Valentine and Frank G. Vallee, editors. McClelland and Stewart Limited, Toronto, 1971.

Kleinfeld, Judith. "Visual Memory In Village Eskimo And Urban Caucasian Children." In Arctic, Journal of The Arctic Institute of North America. Vol. 26, No. 3. Montreal, September 1973.

Larsen, Henry A. "The Big Ship." McClelland and Stewart Limited. Toronto, 1967.

Low, A.P. "The Cruise Of The Neptune (Report On The Dominion Government Expedition To Hudson Bay And The Arctic Islands On Board The D.G.S. Neptune 1903-1904." Government Printing Bureau. Ottawa, 1906.

Manker, Ernst. "People Of Eight Seasons." Crescent Books. New York, 1972.

Manning, Mrs. T. "Igloo For The Night." The University Of Toronto Press. Toronto, 1946.

Martijn, Charles A. "Canadian Eskimo Carving In Historical Perspective." In "Eskimo Of The Canadian Arctic," Victor F. Valentine and Frank G. Vallee, editors. McClelland and Stewart Limited. Toronto, 1971.

Marsh, Winifred P. "People Of The Willow." Oxford University Press. Toronto, 1976.

M'Clintock, Francis L. "The Voyage Of The Fox In The Arctic Seas; A Narrative Of The Discovery Of The Fate Of Sir John Franklin And His Companions." John Murray. London, 1859. Reprinted by Hurtig Publishers. Edmonton, 1972.

McKinlay, William L. "Karluk." Weidenfeld and Nicolson. London, 1976.

Metayer, Maurice, editor. "I, Nuligak." Peter Martin Associates Ltd. 1966.

Murdoch, John. "Ethnological Results Of The Point Barrow Expedition." Ninth Annual Report Of The Bureau of Ethnology to the Secretary of the Smithsonian Institution 1887-1888. Government Printing Office. Washington, 1892.

Nansen, Fridtjof. "Farthest North." Harper & Brothers. New York, 1897.

Parry, William E. "Journal Of A Voyage For The Discovery Of A North-West Passage From The Atlantic To The Pacific Performed In The Years 1819-1820 In His Majesty's Ships Hecla And Griper." John Murray. London, 1821. Reprinted by Greenwood Press, Publishers. New York, 1968.

Peacock, F. W. "Some Psychological Aspects Of The Impact Of The White Man Upon The Labrador Eskimos." Unpublished manuscript.

Pitseolak, Peter and Eber, Dorothy. "People From Our Side." Hurtig Publishers. Edmonton, 1975.

Pryde, Duncan. "Nunaga." Walker and Co. New York, 1972.

Rasmussen, Knud. "Intellectual Culture Of The Igloolik Eskimos." Report of the Fifth Thule Expedition 1921-1924, Vol. VII, No. 1. Gyldendalske Boghandel, Nordisk Forlag. Copenhagen, 1929.

Rasmussen, Knud. "Observations On The Intellectual Culture Of The Caribou Eskimos." Report of the Fifth Thule Expedition 1921-1924, Vol. VII, No. 2. Gyldendalske Boghandel, Nordisk Forlag. Copenhagen, 1930.

Rasmussen, Knud. "The Netsilik Eskimos (Social Life And Spiritual Culture)." Report of the Fifth Thule Expedition 1921-1924, Vol. VIII, No. 1-2. Gyldendalske Boghandel, Nordisk Forlag. Copenhagen, 1931.

Rasmussen, Knud. "Intellectual Culture Of The Copper Eskimos." Report of the Fifth Thule Expedition 1921-1924, Vol. IX. Gyldendalske Boghandel, Nordisk Forlag. Copenhagen, 1932.

Rasmussen, Knud. "The Mackenzie Eskimos." H. Osterman, ed. Report of the Fifth Thule Expedition 1921-1924, Vol. X, No. 2. Gyldendalske Boghandel, Nordisk Forlag. Copenhagen, 1942.

Rasmussen, Knud. "Eskimo Poems From Canada And Greenland." University of Pittsburgh Press, Pittsburgh, 1973.

Rink, Henry. "Tales And Traditions Of The Eskimo." William Blackwood and Sons. Edinburgh 1875.

Ross, John. "A Voyage Of Discovery, Made Under The Orders Of The Admiralty, In His Majesty's Ships Isabella And Alexander For The Purpose Of Exploring Baffin's Bay, And Inquiring Into The Probability Of A Northwest Passage." John Murray. London 1819.

Stefansson, Vilhjalmur. "The Friendly Arctic." The Macmillan Company. New York, 1921.

Stefansson, Vilhjalmur. "The Three Voyages Of Martin Frobisher." The Argonaut Press. London, 1938.

Stefansson, Vilhjalmur. "The Fat Of The Land." The Macmillan Company. New York, 1956.

Stefansson, Vilhjalmur. "Cancer: Disease Of Civilization?" Hill and Wang. New York. 1960.

Swinton, George. "Sculpture Of The Eskimo." McClelland and Stewart Limited. Toronto, 1972.

Turquetil, Arsène. "Religious Rituals And Beliefs." In "Eskimo Of The Canadian Arctic," Victor F. Valentine and Frank G. Vallee, editors. McClelland and Stewart Limited. Toronto, 1971.

Valentine, Victor F. and Vallee, Frank G., editors. "Eskimo Of The Canadian Arctic." McClelland and Stewart Limited. Toronto, 1971.

Vallee, Frank G. "Differentiation Among The Eskimo In Some Canadian Arctic Settlements." In "Eskimo Of The Canadian Arctic," Victor F. Valentine and Frank G. Vallee, editors. McClelland and Stewart Limited. Toronto, 1971.

Van Den Steenhoven, Geert. "Caribou Eskimo Legal Concepts." In "Eskimo Of The Canadian Arctic," Victor F. Valentine and Frank G. Vallee, editors. McClelland and Stewart Limited. Toronto, 1971.

Wernick, Robert and the Editors of Time-Life Books. "The Family." Time-Life Books. New York, 1974.

Wilkinson, Doug. "Land Of The Long Day." Clarke, Irwin & Company Ltd. Toronto, 1955.

Index to Photographs

158

Page 75: On a fall evening at low tide, Polar Eskimo children in Greenland play on the glistening rocks near shore.

Page 76: A little girl tries to get the marrow out of a bone.

Page 77: (upper left) Caribou marrow, raw or boiled, is a favorite delicacy. Bones are cracked and the marrow is extracted. (upper right) A berry picker on Hudson Strait gives a sprig of crowberries to her child in the 'amaut'. (lower left) Eskimo family cleaning whitefish; some help, some prefer to watch. (lower right) Helped by his wife and son, a Polar Eskimo in northwest Greenland cuts up a white whale.

Pages 78 and 79: Two straw-blond Lapp girls in Finnish Lapland.

Pages 80 and 81: Indian children play at Tadoule Lake in northern Manitoba.

Page 82: A pensive Eskimo girl on a bus in a northern settlement on Baffin Island.

Page 83: A reflective Eskimo girl, all dressed to play outside, waits patiently for a friend to get ready and join her.

Page 84: Mother and son on a gravel ridge near their Bathurst Inlet camp in the warm light of the arctic spring night.

Page 85: Lapp mother and her baby in their tent.

Page 86: Travel in spring: a little Polar Eskimo boy brings his father's gloves and binoculars to the sled.

Page 87: (upper left) A Polar Eskimo boy of northwest Greenland wears 'nanut', pants made of polar bear fur. (upper right) An Eskimo child during a spring festival at Baker Lake in the central Canadian Arctic. (lower left) A very unhappy little Chipewyan girl. (lower right) A shy little Eskimo girl from the central Arctic.

Page 88: Two little friends set out from their Bathurst Inlet camp.

Page 89: Picking berries in the fall; Baffin Island.

Page 90: An Eskimo girl works on her composition in a school at Repulse Bay in the eastern Canadian Arctic.

Page 99: Lapps walk home from their church in Kautokeino, Norwegian Lapland, after the service.

Pages 100 and 101: A Lapp family in Finnish Lapland.

Page 102: (left) A bright blond Lapp boy in national dress. (right) A little Lapp girl in Norwegian Lapland.

Page 103: (left) An Indian girl at Rupert's House. (right) An Eskimo girl squints in the brilliant light of spring on Jens Munk Island.

Pages 104 and 105: Eskimo family holding service at home on Sunday.

Page 106: An Indian boy from Rupert's House on the James Bay coast, intent on making a drawing in school.

Page 107: An Eskimo boy from Resolute Bay concentrates on his schoolwork.

Pages 108 and 109: Story telling time in a Repulse Bay school for Eskimo children in the far north.

Page 110: (upper left) Lapps read the Bible on Sunday. (upper right) Eskimo mother and child at an Anglican service on Broughton Island. (lower left) While her elders pray, a pensive Indian girl stands in the doorway of the church on an Ontario Indian reserve. (lower right) A little Eskimo girl with her father in a Moravian church on the Labrador coast.

Page 111: Eskimo children romp outside during recess at a school in Grise Fiord in the Canadian Arctic.

Pages 112 and 113: Eskimo children in a high arctic school in Grise Fiord on Ellesmere Island learn about far-off lands.

Page 114: A little boy plays with a pet pup; Bathurst Inlet.

Page 123: An Eskimo woman in northwest Greenland lashes a sealskin cover over the skeleton of a new kayak. Her daughter tries to help.

Pages 124 and 125: An Eskimo boy on Ellesmere Island ices the runners of the long sled.

Pages 126 and 127: Children help their parents to skin a walrus on the shore of northwest Greenland.

Page 128: A Baker Lake Eskimo father teaches his son to spot caribou with a telescope.

Page 129: On Little Diomede Island, an Eskimo boy hunts auklets with his slingshot.

Page 130: A Polar Eskimo boy shoots an arrow into the air with a bow his father made for him.

Page 131: A Lapp boy ties on his boots.

Pages 132 and 133: Children on Little Diomede Island try to catch gulls. In the background is Siberia.

Pages 134 and 135: Children on Cornwallis Island have a snowball fight among the wave-sculptured ice floes pushed onto the shore by the wind.

Page 136: (above) On a trip, an Eskimo father has many duties to perform. (lower left) Immensely fond of small children, most Eskimo men love to play with them. (lower right) A sponge-bath in a chilly tent during a trip near Bathurst Inlet.

Page 137: (clockwise from left) An Eskimo boy from northern Baffin Island. Watched by her little boy, an Eskimo woman cleans a sealskin with her 'ulu', the crescent-shaped woman's knife. An ivory carver on Little Diomede Island is attentively watched by his grandson. An Eskimo girl fills the tea kettle. An Eskimo girl on Little Diomede Island, between Alaska and Siberia. A Chipewyan boy at Tadoule Lake in northernmost Manitoba. The father gets the canoe ready for a trip; the little Eskimo girl carries the baby and the chamber pot.

Page 138: The Lapp baby is kept in the 'komsa', a cradle carved of wood, covered with leather and lined with soft fur.

Page 147: A happy Eskimo girl on Little Diomede Island.

Pages 148 and 149: Travel in spring along smooth ice between sea and land in northwest Greenland; the eldest boy wields the whip, the other children walk behind the sled with their father.

Pages 150 and 151: (from left) A little Eskimo girl with her pet pup. Three Eskimo girls from Grise Fiord in the Northwest Territories with their pet pups. In his imagination, a little boy drives a dogteam like his father. An Eskimo boy romps with a friendly husky; Ward Inlet, Baffin Island.

Pages 152 and 153: Eskimo camp at Bathurst Inlet in fall under a full moon.

Page 154: An Eskimo boy at the entrance to a snow house, warmly dressed for a day of playing on Jens Munk Island.